NUTCA

EUROPEAN UNION
LAW

AUSTRALIA
LBC Information Services
Sydney

CANADA and USA
Carswell
Toronto · Ontario

NEW ZEALAND
Brooker's
Auckland

SINGAPORE and MALAYSIA
Thomson Information (S.E. Asia)
Singapore

NUTCASES

EUROPEAN UNION LAW

FIRST EDITION

by

PENELOPE KENT
LLB, LLM, Solicitor
Principal Lecturer
School of Law, Middlesex University

London · Hong Kong · Dublin
Sweet & Maxwell
1997

Published in 1997 by
Sweet & Maxwell Limited
of 100 Avenue Road
London, NW3 3PF

Phototypeset by J&L Composition Ltd, Filey, North Yorkshire
Printed in England by Clays Ltd, St Ives plc

No natural forests were destroyed to make this product:
only farmed timber was used and re-planted

ISBN 0 421 596902

**A CIP catalogue record for this book is available
from the British Library**

CONTENTS

Table of Cases   vii
Table of Commission Decisions   xviii
Table of Abbreviations   xix

1. The legal order of the E.C. and E.U.   1
2. The institutions of the E.C. and E.U.   15
3. Fundamental rights and general
        principles   21
4. Enforcement of E.C. law   28
5. Judicial review of the acts of the
        E.C. institutions   35
6. Liability of the E.C. institutions   44
7. Preliminary rulings   51
8. Free movement of goods   59
9. Free movement of capital   73
10. Free movement of workers   75
11. Right of establishment and freedom
        to provide services   89
12. Competition law 1: agreements and
        restrictive practices under Article
        85   98
13. Competition law 2: abuse of a
        dominant position under article 86   110
14. Equal pay and treatment   123

Index   139

TABLE OF CASES

ACF Chemiefarma v. Commission (E.C.) (Case 41/69) [1970]
    E.C.R. 661.. **99**
AKZO Chemie BV v. Commission (E.C.) (Case 62/86) [1986]
    E.C.R. 1965; [1986] 3 C.M.L.R. 273................ **116**, 117
Adams v. Commission (E.C.) (Case 145/83) [1985] E.C.R. 3539;
    [1986] 1 C.M.L.R. 506........................... **50, 121**
Adoui and Cornuaille v. Belgian State (Cases 115–116/81); [1982]
    E.C.R. 1665; [1982] 3 C.M.L.R. 631.................... 87
Ahlstrom (A.) OY v. Commission (E.C.) ("Woodpulp") (Cases
    C 89, 104, 114, 116–117 & 125–129/85); [1993]
    E.C.R. I–1307; [1993] 4 C.M.L.R. 407 .... 101, 105, 114
Alpine Investments B.V. v. Minister Van Financien (Case C-384/93)
    [1995] E.C.R. I–1141; [1995] 2 C.M.L.R. 209 .... **95**
Apple and Pear Development Council v. Lewis (Case 222/82) [1983]
    E.C.R. 4083; [1984] 3 C.M.L.R. 733.................... 63
Atkins v. Wrekin District Council (Case C-228/94) [1996] 3
    C.M.L.R. 863....................................... 138
Australian Mining & Smelting Co. Ltd v. Commission (E.C.)
    (Case 155/79) [1982] E.C.R. 1575; [1982] 2 C.M.L.R. 264 ... 121

BAT and Reynolds v. Commission (E.C.) (Cases 142 & 156/84)
    [1985] E.C.R. 363; [1987] 2 C.M.L.R. 551 118
BMW Belgium SA v. Commission (E.C.) (Cases 32/78 &
    36–82/78) [1979] E.C.R. 2435; [1980] 1 C.M.L.R. 370 116
Barber v. Guardian Royal Exchange (Case C-262/88) [1990]
    E.C.R.I-1889; [1990] 2 C.M.L.R. 513 ..... 7, 124, **125**, 126, **128**,
    .... 131, 138
Barra v. Belgium and City of Liege (Case 309/85) [1988] E.C.R. 355;
    [1989] 1 C.M.L.R. 337.............................. 98
Bayerische HNL v. Council (E.C.) and Commission (E.C.)
    (Cases 83 & 94/76 and 4, 15 & 40/77) [1978] E.C.R. 1029;
    [1978] 3 C.M.L.R. 566............................ 47, **48**
Belgapom v. ITM Belgium and Vocarex SA (Case C-63/94) [1995]
    E.C.R. I–2467 66
Bethell v. Commission (E.C.) (Case 246/81) [1982] E.C.R. 2277;
    [1982] 3 C.M.L.R. 300; [1985] E.C.R. 1; [1985] 2 C.M.L.R.
    286 .... **43**
Bettray v. Staatssecretaris van Justitie (Case 344/87) [1989] E.C.R.
    1621; [1991] 1 C.M.L.R. 459 76
Bilka Kaufhaus v. Weber von Hartz (Case 170/84) [1986] 5 E.C.R.
    1607; [1986] 2 C.M.L.R. 701 .... 124, **126**, 127, **129**

Blaizot v. University of Liège (Case 24/86); [1988] E.C.R. 379;
 [1989] 1 C.M.L.R. 57 98
Bonsignore v. Oberstadtdirektor der Stadt Köln (Case 67/74) [1975]
 E.C.R. 297; [1975] 1 C.M.L.R. 472 88
Brasserie du Pêcheur SA v. Germany (Case C-46/93) [1996] 1
 C.M.L.R. 889 . . . . **12**, 13, 14
British Aerospace and Rover Group Holdings plc v. Commission
 (E.C.) (Case C-294/90) [1992] E.C.R. I-493 . . . . **33**, 34
Broekmeulen v. Huisarts Registratie Commissie (Case 246/80)
 [1981] E.C.R. 2311; [1982] 1 C.M.L.R. 91 . . . . **53**
Brown v. Secretary of State for Scotland (Case 197/86) [1988]
 E.C.R. 3205; [1988] C.M.L.R. 403 . . . . 84, 98
Brunner v. E.U. Treaty [1994] 1 C.M.L.R. 57 22
Bulmer v. Bollinger [1974] 2 All E.R. 1226, CA. 54
Burgoin v. MAFF [1985] 3 All E.R. 458, CA 71
Burton v. British Railways Board (Case 19/81) [1982] E.C.R. 555;
 [1982] 2 C.M.L.R. 136 128

CILFIT Srl v. Minister of Health (Case 283/81) [1982] E.C.R. 3415;
 [1983] 1 C.M.L.R. 472 . . . . **54**
CNTA v. Commission (E.C.) (Case 74/74) [1975] E.C.R. 533 . . . . **47**, **49**
Campo Ebro Industrial v. Council (E.C.) (Case T-472/93) [1995]
 E.C.R. II-421; [1996] 1 C.M.L.R. 267 40
Campus Oil v. Minister for Industry and Energy (Case 72/83) [1983]
 E.C.R. 2727; [1984] 3 C.M.L.R. 544 . . . . **70**
Carvel & Guardian Newspapers v. Council (Case T-194/94)
 [1995] C.M.L.R. 359 . . . . **20**, 21
Casagrande v. Londeshauptstadt Munchen (Case 9/74) [1974]
 E.C.R. 773; [1974] 2 C.M.L.R. 423 . . . . **84**
Cassis de Dijon. *See* Rewe Zentrale AG v. Bundesmonopolverwaltung
 fur Branntwein
Castelli v. ONPTS (Case 261/83) [1984] E.C.R. 3199; [1987] 1
 C.M.L.R. 465 83
Chernobyl. *See* European Parliament v. Council (E.C.) (Case C-70/88)
Cimenteries v. Commission (E.C.) (Noordwijk's Cement Accord)
 (Cases 8–11/66) [1967] E.C.R. 75 . . . . **36**
Codorniu v. Council (E.C.) (Case C-309/89); [1994] E.C.R. I-1853 . . **40**
Colegio Oficial de Agentas de la Propriedad Immobiliara v.
 Aguirre, Newman and others (Case C-104/91) [1992]
 E.C.R. I-3003 . . . . **93**
Coloroll Pension Trustees v. Russell (Case C-200/91) [1994] E.C.R.
 I-4389; [1995] All E.R. (E.C.) 23 126
Comitology. *See* European Parliament v. Council (Case 302/87)
Commercial Solvents v. Commission (E.C.) (Joined Cases 6–7/73)
 [1974] E.C.R. 223 116
Commission (E.C.) v. BASF (Case C-137/92P) [1994] E.C.R. I-2555 . **37**
Commission (E.C.) v. Belgium (*Re* Public Employees) (Case 149/79)
 [1982] E.C.R. 1845; [1981] 2 C.M.L.R. 413 . . . . **85**
Commission (E.C.) v. Council (E.C.) (Re ERTA) (Case 22/70),
 [1971] E.C.R. 263; [1971] C.M.L.R. 335 36

Commission (E.C.) v. Council (E.C.) (Case 45/86) [1987] E.C.R.
1493 .... **17**, 41
Commission (E.C.) v. Council (E.C.) (Case C-300/89) [1991]
E.C.R. I–2867 .... **18**
Commission (E.C.) v. Denmark (Case 302/86) [1988] E.C.R. 4607;
[1989] 1 C.M.L.R. 619............................ **64**
Commission (E.C.) v. France (Case 196/85) [1987] E.C.R. 1597;
[1988] 2 C.M.L.R. 851............................ 60
Commission (E.C.) v. France (Case C-154/89) [1991] E.C.R. I–659.... 92
Commission (E.C.) v. Germany (Case 205/84) [1986] E.C.R. 3755;
[1987] 2 C.M.L.R. 69............................ **91**, 93
Commission (E.C.) v. Germany (Case 178/84) [1987] E.C.R. 1227;
[1988] 1 C.M.L.R. 780.......................... 13, 64, 70
Commission (E.C.) v. Germany (Case 249/86) [1989] E.C.R. 1263;
[1990] 3 C.M.L.R. 540............................ **77**
Commission (E.C.) v. Greece (Case 272/86) [1988] E.C.R. 4875..... **29**
Commission (E.C.) v. Greece (Case C-189/89) [1991] E.C.R. I–727 .. **92**
Commission (E.C.) v. Greece (Case C-120/94R) [1994] E.C.R.
I–3037... **34**
Commission (E.C.) v. Ireland (Case 249/81) [1982] E.C.R. 4005..... **62**
Commission (E.C.) v. Italy (Pigmeat) (Case 7/61) [1961] E.C.R.
317; [1962] C.M.L.R. 39.......................... 30, 37
Commission (E.C.) v. Italy (Export Tax on Art Treasures) (Case 7/68)
[1968] E.C.R. 423; [1969] C.M.L.R. 1 72
Commission (E.C.) v. Italy (Case 31/69) [1970] E.C.R. 25; [1970]
C.M.L.R. 175.................................... **29**, 30
Commission (E.C.) v. Italy (Case 28/81) [1981] E.C.R. 2577......... 32
Commission (E.C.) v. Italy (Case 163/82) [1982] E.C.R. 3273....... 136
Commission (E.C.) v. Italy (Case 101/84) [1985] E.C.R. 2629;
[1986] 2 C.M.L.R. 352............................ **30**
Commission (E.C.) v. Italy (Case 22/87) [1989] E.C.R. 143
Commission (E.C.) v. Luxembourg (Case C-473/93) [1996] 3
C.M.L.R. 981.................................... 86
Commission (E.C.) v. Spain (Case C-45/93) [1994] E.C.R. I–911 96
Commission (E.C.) v. United Kingdom (Case 128/78) [1979]
E.C.R. 419; [1979] 2 C.M.L.R. 45 .... **31**
Commission (E.C.) v. United Kingdom (*Re* Excise Duties on Wine)
(No. 1) (Case 170/78) [1980] E.C.R. 417; [1983] 3 C.M.L.R.
512 .... **60**
Commission (E.C.) v. United Kingdom (*Re* Excise Duties on Wine)
(No. 2) (Case 170/78A) [1983] E.C.R. 2265; [1983] 3
C.M.L.R. 512.................................... 60
Commission (E.C.) v. United Kingdom (*Re* Equal Pay for Equal Work)
(Case 61/81); [1982] E.C.R. 2601; [1982] 3 C.M.L.R. 284... **131**
Commission (E.C.) v. United Kingdom (Case 40/82) [1982] E.C.R.
2793; [1982] 3 C.M.L.R. 497; [1984] E.C.R. 283........... **71**
Commission (E.C.) v. United Kingdom (*Re* Equal Treatment of
Men and Women) (Case 165/82) [1983] E.C.R. 3431;
[1984] 1 C.M.L.R. 44............................ **135**
Commission (E.C.) v. United Kingdom (Case C-246/89) [1991]
E.C.R. 3125.................................... 90

Commission (E.C.) v. United Kingdom (Case 221/89R) [1991]
  E.C.R. I–4585 . . . . **32**
Commission (E.C.) v. United Kingdom (Case C-246/89R) [1991]
  E.C.R. I–45985 5
Conegate Ltd v. H.M. Customs and Excise (Case 121/85) [1986]
  E.C.R. 1007; [1986] 2 All E.R. 688 69
Conforama. *See* Union Departmentale des Syndicats CGT de l'Aisne
  v. Sidef Conforama
Consten and Grundig v. Commission (E.C.) (Joined Cases 56 &
  58/64) [1966] E.C.R. 299; [1966] C.M.L.R. 418
  . . . . **102**, 103, **106, 108**
Continental Can. *See* Europemballage Corporation and Continental
  Can Co. Inc. v. Commission (E.C.)
Corsica Ferries v. Corpo dei Piloti del Porto di Genova (Case
  C-18/93) [1994] E.C.R. I–1783 114
Costa v. ENEL (Case 6/64) [1964] E.C.R. 585; [1964] C.M.L.R.
  425 . . . . **4, 55**
Cowan v. Tresor Public (Case 186/87) [1989] E.C.R. 195;
  [1990] 2 C.M.L.R. 613 . . . . 26, 96
Cullet v. Centre Leclerc (Case 231/83) [1985] E.C.R. 305;
  1985] 2 C.M.L.R. 524 69
Customs and Excise Commissioners v. Samex [1983] 3 C.M.L.R. 194 . . 52
Customs and Excise Commissioners v. Schindler (Case C-275/92)
  [1994] E.C.R. I–1039; 1 C.M.L.R. 4 95
Cutsforth v. Mansfield Inns [1986] 1 C.M.L.R. 1; [1986] 1 W.L.R.
  558 . . . . **122**

Da Costa en Schaake N.V. v Nederlandse Belastagingadministratie
  (Case 28–30/62) [1963] E.C.R. 31; [1963] C.M.L.R. 224 . . . . . **56**
Danfoss. See Handels-Og Kontorfunktion-aerernesforbund v. Dansk
  Arbeejdsgiverforening for Danfoss
Dassonville. *See* Procureur du Roi v. Dassonville
Defrenne v. Belgian State (No. 1) (Case 80/70) [1971] E.C.R. 445;
  [1971] 1 C.M.L.R. 494 124
Defrenne v. Sabena (No. 2) (Case 43/75) [1976] E.C.R. 4545;
  [1976] 2 C.M.L.R. 98 . . . . **7, 123**, 126
Dekker v. Stichting Vormingscentrum voor Jonge Volvassenen Plus
  (Case C-177/88) [1990] E.C.R. I–3841; [1991] 1 R.L.R. 27
  . . . . 127, **132**
Delimitis v. Henninger Vrau (Case C-234/89) [1991] E.C.R. I–935;
  [1992] 5 C.M.L.R. 210 . . . . **104**, 107
Diatta v. Land Berlin (Case 267/83) [1985] E.C.R. 567; [1986] 2
  C.M.L.R. 164 . . . . **78**, 79
Dietz v. Stichtung Thuiszorg Rotterdam (Case C-435/93) [1997] 1
  C.M.L.R. 119 . . . . **127**, 128
Dona v. Mantero (Case 13/76) [1976] E.C.R. 1333 81
Dow Benelux N.V. v. Commission (E.C.) (Case 85/87) [1989]
  E.C.R. 3137 120
Duke v. Reliance Systems (1983) [1988] A.C. 618; [1987] 2 C.M.L.R.
  24 11

Dumortier Frères SA v. Council (Cases 64 & 113/76; 167 & 239/78; 27–28 & 45/79) [1982] E.C.R. 1733; [1979] E.C.R. 3091 50
Dyestuffs. *See* Imperial Chemical Industries Ltd v. Commission (E.C.)
Dzodzi v. Belgium (Joined Cases C 297/88 & 197/89) [1990] E.C.R. I–3763 57

EMI Electrola v. Patricia (Case 341/87) [1989] E.C.R. 79; [1989] 2 C.M.L.R. 413 . . . . **72**
El Corte Ingles SA v. Rivero (Case C-192/94) [1996] E.C.R. I–1296. . . 8
Enderby v. Frenchay Area Health Authority and Secretary of State for Health (Case C-127/92) [1993] E.C.R. I–5535 [1994] 1 All E.R. 495 129
European Parliament v. Council (E.C.) (Case 13/83) [1985] E.C.R. 1513; [1986] 1 C.M.L.R. 138 . . . . **16**, 20, **42**
European Parliament v. Council (E.C.) ("Comitology") (Case 302/87) [1988] E.C.R. 5615 38
European Parliament v. Council (E.C.) ("Chernobyl") (Case C-70/88) [1990] E.C.R. I–2041 . . . . **37**, 38
European Parliament v. Council (E.C.) (*Re* Students' Rights) (Case C-295/90) [1991] 1 E.C.R. 4193; [1992] 3 C.M.L.R. 281 . . . . **16**
Europemballage Corporation and Continental Can Co. Inc. v. Commission (E.C.) ("Continental Can") (Case 6/72) [1973] E.C.R. 495; [1973] C.M.L.R. 199 . . . . **111**, 112, **117**

Faccini Dori v. Recreb (Case C-91/92) [1994] E.C.R. I–3325; [1995] All E.R. (E.C.) 1 8
Fiorini (Cristini) v. SNCF (Case 32/75) [1975] E.C.R. 1085; [1975] 1 C.M.L.R. 573 . . . . **82**
Fisscher v. Voorhuis Hengelo (Case C-128/93) [1994] E.C.R. I–4583 . 128
Foglia v. Novella (No. 1) (Case 104/79) [1980] E.C.R. 745, [1981] 1 C.M.L.R. 45. . . . . **56**, 57
Foglia v. Novella (No. 2) (Case 244/80) [1981] E.C.R. 3045; [1982] 1 C.M.L.R. 585 57
Foster v. British Gas (Case C-188/89) [1990] E.C.R. I–3133; [1990] 2 C.M.L.R. 833 8
Foto-Frost v. Hauptzollamt Lubeck-Ost (Case 314/85) [1987] E.C.R. 4199; [1988] 3 C.M.L.R. 57 . . . . **57**, 58
France v. Commission (E.C.) (Case C-303/90); [1991] E.C.R. I–2223. 36
France v. United Kingdom (*Re* Fishing Net Mesh Sizes) (Case 141/78) [1979] E.C.R. 2923; [1980] 1 C.M.L.R. 6 . . . . 32, 33
Francovich, Bonifaci and Others v. Italy (Cases C 6 & 9/90) [1991] E.C.R. I–5357; [1993] 2 C.M.L.R. 66 . . . . 10, **11**, 12, 13, 15, ... 29, 47, 122

Garden Cottage Foods v. Milk Marketing Board [1983] 3 C.M.L.R. 43, HL 122
Garland v. BREL (Case 12/81) [1982] E.C.R. 359; [1982] 1 C.M.L.R. 696. 124

Gebhard v. Consiglio Dell 'Ordrine Degli Avvocat: Procurator di
   Milano (Case C-55/94) [1996] All E.R. (E.C.) 189 91
Germany v. Commission (E.C.) (*Re* Tariff Quotas on Wine)
   (Case 24/62) [1963] E.C.R. 63; [1963] C.M.L.R. 347. 41
Germany, France, Netherlands, Denmark and the United
   Kingdom v. Commission (E.C.) (Joined Cases 281, 283, 287/85)
   [1987] E.C.R. 3203 . . . . **19**
Grad v. Finanzamt Traunstein (Case 9/70) [1970] E.C.R. 825. . . . . **6**
Gravier v. City of Liege (Case 293/83) [1985] E.C.R. 593;
   [1985] 3 C.M.L.R. 1. . . . . **97**, 98
Groener v. Minister for Education (Case 397/87) [1989] E.C.R.
   3967; [1990] 1 C.M.L.R. 401 80
Groenveld v. Produktschap voor Vee en Vlees (Case 15/79) [1979]
   E.C.R. 3967; [1981] 1 C.M.L.R. 207. . . . . **67**

Haegeman v. Commission (E.C.) (Case 96/71) [1973] E.C.R. 449;
   • [1973] C.M.L.R. 365 51
Haim v. Kassenzahnarttliche Vereinigun Nordhein (Case C-319/92)
   [1994] E.C.R. I–425; [1994] 2 C.M.L.R. 169. . . . . **94**
Handels-Og Kontorfunktionaernesforbund v. Dansk Arbeejdsgiverforening
   for Danfoss ("Danfoss") (Case 109/88) [1989] E.C.R. I–3979;
   [1991] 1 C.M.L.R. 8. 131
Handels-Og Kontorfunktionaerer-Nes Forbund I Danmark (Acting
   for Hertz) v. Dansk Arbeejdsgiverforening (Case C-179/88)
   [1990] E.C.R. I–3979; [1992] I.C.R. 332. 132
Hilti v. Commission (E.C.) (Case C-53/92) [1994] E.C.R. I–667 113
Hoechst v. Commission (E.C.) (Cases 46/87 & 227/88) [1989]
   E.C.R. 2859; [1991] 4 C.M.L.R. 410. 120
Hoffman – La Roche v. Commission (E.C.) ("Vitamins") (Case 85/76)
   [1979] E.C.R. 461; [1979] 3 C.M.L.R. 211 . . . . **110**, 113, 115
Hofmann v. Barmer Ersatzkasse (Case 184/83) [1984] E.C.R. 3042;
   [1986] 1 C.M.L.R. 242. 136
Hugin-Kassaregister A.B. v. Commission (E.C.) (Case 22/78) [1979]
   E.C.R. 1869; [1979] 3 C.M.L.R. 345. 113
Humblot v. Directeur des Services Fiscaux [1986] 2 C.M.L.R. 338 61
Hunermund v. Landesapothekerkammer Baden-Wurttemburg (Case
   C-292/92) [1993] E.C.R. I–6787. 66

Imperial Chemical Industries Ltd v. Commission (E.C.) ("Dyestuffs")
   (Case 48/69) [1972] E.C.R. 619 . . . . **100**, 101, **105**
International Fruit N.V. (No. 1) v. Commission (E.C.) (Cases
   41–44/70) [1971] E.C.R. 411; [1975] 2 C.M.L.R. 515 . . . . **38**
Internationale Handelsgesellschaft mbH v. Einfuhr-und Vorratsstelle
   fur Getreide und Futtermittel (Case 11/70) [1970] E.C.R.
   1125; [1972] C.M.L.R. 255. . . . . **22**
Italian Minister of Finance v. Simmenthal (Case 106/77) [1978]
   E.C.R. 629. . . . . **4**
Italy v. Council (E.C.) and Commission (E.C.) (Case 32/65) [1966]
   E.C.R. 389; [1969] C.M.L.R. 39. . . . . **43**
Italy v. Sacchi (Case 155/73) [1974] E.C.R. 409. 99

Jenkins v. Kingsgate (Clothing Productions) Ltd (Case 96/80) [1981]
    E.C.R. 911; [1981] 2 C.M.L.R. 24 .... 127, 129
Johnston v. Chief Constable of the Royal Ulster Constabulary (Case
    22/84) [1986] E.C.R. 1651; [1986] 3 C.M.L.R. 240......... **26**

Kalancke v. Frei Hanseatadt Bremen (Case C-450/93) [1996] 1
    C.M.L.R. 175.................................... **136**, 137
Kampffmeyer v. Commission (E.C.) (Case 5/66) [1967] E.C.R.
    245 .... **48, 51**
Keck and Mithouard (Joined Cases C 267–268/91) [1993] E.C.R.
    I–6097; [1995] 1 C.M.L.R. 101............. 56, 62, **66**, 67, 95
Kempf v. Staatssecretaris van Justitie (Case 139/85) [1986] E.C.R.
    1741; [1987] 1 C.M.L.R. 764 76
Kohl v. Ringelhan & Rennett SA (Case 177/83) [1984] E.C.R. 3651;
    [1985] 3 C.M.L.R. 340.............................. 69
Kolpinghuis Nijmegen. *See* Officier van Justitie v. Kolpinghuis Nijmegen
Krohn v. Commission (E.C.) (Case 175/84) [1986] E.C.R. 753;
    [1987] 1 C.M.L.R. 745.............................. 51

Lair v. University of Hanover (Case 39/86) [1988] E.C.R. 3161;
    [1989] 3 C.M.L.R. 545......................... **83**, 84, 98
Lancôme v. Etos B.V. (Perfumes) (Case 99/79) [1980] E.C.R. 2511;
    [1981] C.M.L.R. 164 .... 37, **109**
Lawrie – Blum v. Land Baden Wurttemberg (Case 66/85) [1986]
    E.C.R. 2121; [1987] 3 C.M.L.R. 389.................. **75**
Leonesio v. Italian Minister of Agriculture (Case 93/71) [1972] E.C.R.
    287; [1973] C.M.L.R. 343............................ 6
Levin v. Staatssecretaris van Justitie (Case 53/81) [1982] E.C.R.
    1035; [1982] 2 C.M.L.R. 454 .... **76**
Lucien Ortscheit GmbH v. Eurim-Pharm GmbH (Case C-320/93)
    [1994] E.C.R. I–5243.............................. 71
Luisi and Carbone v. Ministero del Tesoro (Case 286/83) [1984]
    E.C.R. 377; [1985] 3 C.M.L.R. 52 .... **96**
Lütticke v. Commission (E.C.) (Case 4/69) [1971] E.C.R.
    325 .... **44**, 45, 46, 50
Luxembourg v. European Parliament (Case 230/81) [1983] E.C.R.
    255; [1983] 2 C.M.L.R. 726 35

Macarthys Ltd v. Smith (Case 129/79) [1980] E.C.R. 1275;
    [1980] 2 C.M.L.R. 205...................... **129**, 130
Marchandise, *Re* (Case C-332/89) [1991] E.C.R. I–1027; [1993] 3
    C.M.L.R. 746..................................... 65
Marleasing SA v. La Comercial Internacional de Alimentacion SA
    (Case C-106/89) [1990] E.C.R. I–4135; [1992] 1 C.M.L.R.
    305 .... **9**, 10, 11
Marshall v. Southampton and South West Hampshire Area Health
    Authority (No. 1) (Case 152/84) [1986] E.C.R. 723; [1986]
    1 C.M.L.R. 688 .... 78, **134**
Marshall v. Southampton and South West Area Health Authority
    (No. 2) (Case C-271/91) [1993] E.C.R. I–4367; [1993] 3
    C.M.L.R. 293.................................... 135

Metro-SB-Grossmarkte GmbH v. Commission (E.C.) (Case 326/76)
 [1977] E.C.R. 1875; [1978] 2 C.M.L.R. 1 104
Michelin (N.V. Nederlandsche Baden-industrie Michelin) v.
 Commission (E.C.) (Case 322/81) [1983] E.C.R. 3461;
 [1985] 1 C.M.L.R. 282 . . . . **113**, 114
Ministere Public v. Claude Muller and Kampfmeyer-France Sarl
 (Case 304/84) [1986] E.C.R. 1511; [1987] 2 C.M.L.R. 469 70
Ministerio Fiscal v. Aldo Bordessa (Cases C 358 & 416/93) [1995]
 E.C.R. I–361; [1996] 2 C.M.L.R. 13 . . . . **73**, 74
Ministerio Fiscalo v. Emilio (Cases C 163–164 & 250/94)
 [1995] 1 C.M.L.R. 631 . . . . **74**
Morson v. Netherlands (Joined Cases 35–36/82) [1982] E.C.R. 3723;
 [1983] 2 C.M.L.R. 221 76
Mulder v. Council (E.C.) and Commission (E.C.) (Joined Cases C
 104/89 and 37/90) [1992] E.C.R. I–3061 49
Mulder v. Minister van Landbouw en Visserig (Case 120/86) [1988]
 E.C.R. 2321; [1989] 2 C.M.L.R. 1 . . . . **24**
Musique Diffusion Francaise v. Commission (E.C.) (Cases
 100–103/80) [1983] E.C.R. 1825; [1983] 3 C.M.L.R. 221 . . . **121**

National Panasonic (U.K.) Ltd v. Commission (Case 136/79) [1980]
 E.C.R. 2033; [1980] 3 C.M.L.R. 169 . . . . 23, **120**
Neath v. Hugh Steeper (Case C-152/91) [1993] E.C.R. I–6935; [1994]
 1 All E.R. 929 126
Neeltje v. Houtwipper (Case C-293/93) [1994] E.C.R. I–4249;
 [1995] All E.R. (E.C.) 163 . . . . **67**
Netherlands v. Reed (Case 59/85) [1986] E.C.R. 1283; [1987] 2
 C.M.L.R. 448 . . . . **77**
Nold v. Commission (E.C.) (Case 4/73) [1970] E.C.R. 491;
 [1974] 2 C.M.L.R. 338 22
Nordsee Deutsche Hochseefischere GmbH v. Reedere; Mond
 Hochseefisherei Nordstern AG & Co. KG (Case 102/81) [1982]
 E.C.R. 1095 53

Oebel (Sergius) *Re* (Case 155/80) [1981] E.C.R. 1993; [1983] 1
 C.M.L.R. 390 65
Officier van Justitie v. Kolpinghuis Nijmegen (Case 80/86) [1987]
 E.C.R. 3969; [1989] 2 C.M.L.R. 18. 9
Officier van Justitie v. Koninklijke Kaasfabrik Eyssen B.V. (Case
 53/80) [1981] E.C.R. 409; [1982] 2 C.M.L.R. 20. . . . . **70**
Orkem v. Commission (E.C.) (Case 374/87) [1989] E.C.R. 3283 . . 27, 120

Parti Ecologise ("Les Verts") v. European Parliament (Case 294/83)
 [1986] E.C.R. 1339; [1987] 2 C.M.L.R. 343 . . . . **35**, 36
Patrick v. Ministre des Affaires Culturelles (Case 11/77) [1977] E.C.R.
 1199; [1977] 2 C.M.L.R. 523 91
Pigmeat. *See* Commission (E.C.) v. Italy (Case 7/61)
Piraiki-Patraiki v. Commission (E.C.) (Case 11/82) [1985] E.C.R.
 207; [1985] 2 C.M.L.R. 4 39
Plaumann & Co. v. Commission (Case 25/62) [1963] E.C.R. 95;
 [1964] C.M.L.R. 29 . . . . **39**

Procureur du Roi v. Dassonville (Case 8/74) [1974] E.C.R. 837;
    [1974] 2 C.M.L.R. 436 . . . . **61**, 62, 66
Procureur du Roi v. Royer (Case 48/75) [1976] E.C.R. 497;
    [1976] 2 C.M.L.R. 619 . . . . **79**, 88
Pronuption de Paris GmbH Frankfurt am Main v. Schillgalis (Case
    161/84) [1986] 1 E.C.R. 353; [1986] 1 C.M.L.R. 414 . . . 101, 104
Pubblico Ministero v. Ratti (Case 148/78) [1979] E.C.R. 1629;
    [1980] 1 C.M.L.R. 96 . . . . **6**
Publishers' Association v. Commission (E.C.) (Case C-360/92P)
    [1995] E.C.R. I–23; [1995] 5 C.M.L.R. 33 102

RTE, BBC and ITP v. Commission (E.C.) (Case 241/91P) [1995]
    E.C.R. I–801; [1995] All E.R. (E.C.) 416 . . . . 114, **116**
R. v. Bouchereau (Case 30/77) [1977] E.C.R. 1999; [1977] 2
    C.M.L.R. 800 . . . . **87**
R. v. Henn and Darby (Case 34/79) [1979] E.C.R. 3795; [1980] 1
    C.M.L.R. 246; on referral from [1979] 2 C.M.L.R. 495,
    HL. **61**, **68**
R v. H.M. Treasury, ex p. British Telecommunications plc (Case
    C-392/93) [1996] All E.R. (E.C.) 411 . . . . **14**
R. v. Immigration Appeal Tribunal, ex p. Antonissen (Case C-292/89)
    [1991] E.C.R. I–745; [1991] 2 C.M.L.R. 373. 79
R. v. Immigration Appeal Tribunal, ex p. Surinder Singh
    (Case C-370/90) [1991] E.C.R. I-4265. 77
R. v. International Stock Exchange of the U.K. and the Republic of
    Ireland, ex p. Else [1931] 1 All E.R. 420, C.A. 54
R. v. Intervention Board for Agricultural Produce, ex p. Man (Sugar)
    (Case 181/84) [1985] E.C.R. 2889; [1985] 3 C.M.L.R. 759 . . . **24**
R. v. Kirk (Case 63/83) [1984] E.C.R. 2689; [1984] 3 C.M.L.R. 522 . **23**
R. v. Minister of Agriculture, Fisheries and Food, ex p. Hedley
    Lomas (Ireland) Ltd (Case C-5/94) [1996] All E.R. (E.C.)
    493 . . . . **14**, 15
R. v. Secretary of State for Employment, ex p. Equal
    Opportunities Commission [1995] 1 A.C. 1; [1994] 2 W.L.R.
    409 . . . . **124**, 127
R. v. Secretary of State for Health, ex p. Richardsons (Case
    C-137/94) [1995] 3 C.M.L.R. 376. 138
R. v. Secretary of State for the Home Department, ex p. Sandhu
    The Times, May 10, 1985 78
R. v. Secretary of State for Social Security, ex p. Smithson (Case
    C-243/90) [1992] E.C.R. I–467; [1992] 1 C.M.L.R. 1061. 138
R. v. Secretary of State for Transport, ex p. Factortame (No.2) (Case
    C-213/89) [1990] E.C.R. I–2433; [1990] 3 C.M.L.R.
    375 . . . . **5**, 13, 58
R. v. Secretary of State for Transport, ex p. Factortame (No.3) (Case
    C-48/93) [1991] 3 C.M.L.R. 589; [1996] 1 C.M.L.R.
    889 . . . . **5**, 12, 13, 14, 90
R. v. Secretary of State for Transport, ex p. Factortame (No. 5) (QBD)
    The Times, September 11, 1997 13
R. v. Thompson and Others (Case 7/78) [1978] E.C.R. 2247;
    [1979] 1 C.M.L.R. 47. . . . . **69**

Reina v. Landeskreditbank Baden-Wurttemberg (Case 65/81) [1982]
    E.C.R. 33; [1982] 1 C.M.L.R. 744 83
Remia and Nutricia v. Commission (E.C.) (Case 42/84) [1985] 6
    E.C.R. 2545; [1987] 1 C.M.L.R. 1 104
Rewe Zentrale AG v. Bundesmonopolverwaltung fur Branntwein
    ("Cassis de Dijon") (Case 120/78) [1979] E.C.R. 649;
    [1979] 3 C.M.L.R. 494 . . . . 25, **63**, 64, 66, 67, 93
Reyners v. Belgian State (Case 2/74) [1974] E.C.R. 631; [1974]
    2 C.M.L.R. 305 . . . . **89**, 90
Rheinmullen Dusseldorf v. Einfuhr-und Vorratsstelle fur Getreide
    und Futtermittel (Joined Cases 146 & 166/73) [1974]
    E.C.R. 33; [1974] 1 C.M.L.R. 523 . . . . **51**
Richez-Parise v. Commission (Case 19/69) [1970] E.C.R. 325 . . . . **45**
Rinner-Kuhn v. F.W.W. Spezial-Gebaudereinigung GmbH & Co. K.G.
    (Case 171/88) [1989] E.C.R. 2743; [1989] 1 RLR 493 . . . . . . **124**
Roberts v. Tate and Lyle Industries Ltd (Case 151/84) [1986] E.C.R.
    703; [1986] 1 C.M.L.R. 714 134
Roquette Freres v. Council (E.C.) (Case 138/79) [1980] E.C.R.
    3393 . . . . **15**, 16, **41**
Royer. *See* Procureur du Roi v. Royer
Rummler v. Data Druck GmbH (Case 237/85) [1986] E.C.R. 2101;
    [1987] 3 C.M.L.R. 127 . . . . **130**
Rutili v. Minister of the Interior (Case 36/75) [1975] E.C.R. 1219;
    [1976] 1 C.M.L.R. 140 . . . . **88**, 89

S.A. Magnavision N.V. v. General Optical Council (No.1) [1987] 2
    C.M.L.R. 887 55
S.A. Magnavision N.V. v. General Optical Council (No.2) [1987] 2
    C.M.L.R. 262 55
Sabbatini v. European Parliament (Case 20/71) [1972] E.C.R. 345 . . . **25**
Säger v. Dennenmeyer (Case C-76/90); [1991] E.C.R. I-4221 96
Sayag v. Lednc (Case 5/68) [1969] E.C.R. 329 . . . . **45**
Schoppenstedt. *See* Zukerfabrik Schoppenstedt v. Council
Simmenthal v. Commission (E.C.) (Case 92/78) [1979] E.C.R. 777;
    [1980] 1 C.M.L.R. 25 44
Sociaal Fonds voor de Diamantarbeiders v. S.A. C. Brachfeld (Cases
    2-3/69) [1969] E.C.R. 211; [1969] C.M.L.R. 335 . . . . **59**
Societe Technique Miniere v. Maschinenbau Ulm GmbH (Case
    56/65) [1966] E.C.R. 235; [1966] C.M.L.R. 357 . . . . **101, 103**
Society for the Protection of Unborn Children v. Grogan (Case
    C-159/90) [1991] E.C.R. I-4685; [1991] 3 C.M.L.R. 849 . . . 57, **97**
Sofrimport v. Commission (Case C-152/88) [1990] E.C.R. I-2477;
    [1990] 3 C.M.L.R. 80 40
Solvay v. Commission (Case 27/88) [1989] E.C.R. 3355; [1991] 4
    C.M.L.R. 502 27
Sotgiu v. Deutsche Bundespost (Case 152/73) [1974] E.C.R. 153 . . . . . **82**
Spijker Kwasten N.V. v. Commission (E.C.) (Case 231/82) [1983]
    E.C.R. 2559; [1984] 2 C.M.L.R. 284 40
Star Fruit Co. v. Commission (E.C.) (Case 247/87) [1989] E.C.R.
    291; [1990] 1 C.M.L.R. 733 30

Stauder v. City of Ulm (Case 29/69) [1969] E.C.R. 419; [1970]
C.M.L.R. 112. . . . . **21**
Stegmann v. Staatsseretaris van Justitie (Case 196/87) [1988] E.C.R.
6159; [1989] 1 C.M.L.R. 449 76
Stoke-on-Trent and Norwich City Council v. B & Q plc (Case
C-169/91) [1992] E.C.R. I–6635; [1993] 1 C.M.L.R. 426. 65

Tankstation't Heukste Vof and Boermans (Cases C-401–401/92)
[1994] E.C.R. I–2199 66
Ten Oever v. Stichtung Bedriffspensioenfonds Voor Het Glazenwassers
(Case C-109/91) [1993] E.C.R. I–4879 126
Tetra Pak II. *See* Tetra Pak Rausing SA v. Commission (E.C.), (Case
T-83/91)
Tetra Pak Rausing SA v. Commission (E.C.) (Case T-51/89) [1990]
E.C.R. II–309; [1991] 4 C.M.L.R. 334 113
Tetra Pak Rausing SA v. Commission (E.C.) (Case T-83/91) [1994]
E.C.R. II–755. 117
Thieffry v. Couseil de L'Ordre des Avocats a la Cour de Paris (Case
71/76) [1977] E.C.R. 765; [1977] 2 C.M.L.R. 373. 91
Toepfer K.G. v. Commission (E.C.) (Cases 106–107/63) [1965] E.C.R.
405; [1966] C.M.L.R. 111. . . . . **39**
Torfaen Borough Council v. B & Q plc (Case 145/88) [1989] E.C.R.
3851; [1990] 1 C.M.L.R. 337 . . . . **65**
Transocean Marine Paints Association v. Commission (Case 17/74)
[1974] E.C.R. 1063; [1979] 2 C.M.L.R. 459 . . . . 26, **41**

UNECTEF. *See* Union Nationale des Entraineurs et Cadres
Techniques Professionnels du Football v. Heylens
Union Departementale des Syndicats CGT de l'Aisne v. Sidef
Conforama ("Conforama") (Case C-312/89) [1991] E.C.R.
I–997; [1993] 3 C.M.L.R. 746. 65
Union des Associations de Football v. Jean Marc Bosman (Case
C-415/93) [1996] 1 C.M.L.R. 645; [1996] All E.R. (E.C.) 97 . . **81**
Union Nationale des Entraineurs et Cadres Techniques Professionnels
du Football (UNECTEF) v. Heylens (Case 222/86) [1987]
E.C.R. 4097; [1989] 1 C.M.L.R. 901. . . . . 27, 81
United Brands v. Commission (E.C.) (Case 22/76) [1978] E.C.R.
207; [1978] 1 C.M.L.R. 429 . . . . **112**, 113, **114, 115**
United Kingdom v. Commission (E.C.) (*Re* Emergency Measures to
Protect against BSE) (Case C-180/96R) [1996] 3 C.M.L.R.
671 71
United Kingdom v. Council (E.C.) (Case C-84/94) [1996] 3
C.M.L.R. 671. . . . . **27**, 28

VBVB v. Commission (E.C.) (Cases 43 & 63/82) [1984] E.C.R. 19;
[1985] 1 C.M.L.R. 27. 23
Van Binsbergen v. Bestuur van de Bedrifsveerniging voor
de Metaalnijverheied (Case 33/74) [1974] E.C.R. 1299;
[1975] 1 C.M.L.R. 298. . . . . **93**
Van Duyn v. Home Office (No.2) (Case 41/74) [1974] E.C.R. 1337;
[1975] 1 C.M.L.R. 1. . . . . 6, **86**, 87

Van Gend en Loos v. Nederlandse Administratie der Belastingen
    (Case 26/62) [1963] E.C.R. 1; [1963] C.M.L.R. 105 .. 3, 4, 56, **59**
Van Landewyck v. Commission (E.C.) (Cases 209–215 & 218/78);
    [1980] E.C.R. 3125 109
Viho Europe B.V. v. Commission (E.C.) (Case T-102/92) [1995]
    E.C.R. II–17; [1995] All E.R. (E.C.) 371 100
Vlassopoulou v. Ministerium for Justiz, Bundes-und Europaangelegen
    heiten Baden-Wurttemberg (Case C-340/89) [1991] E.C.R.
    I–2357; [1993] 2 C.M.L.R. 221 .... **90**, 91
Volk v. Vervaecke (Case 5/69) [1969] E.C.R. 295; [1969] C.M.L.R.
    273 .... **105**
Von Colson and Kamann v. Land Nordheim-Westfalen (Case 14/83)
    [1994] E.C.R. 1891; [1986] 2 C.M.L.R. 430 .... **8**, 9, 29, **135**
Vroege v. NCIV Institut voor Volkshuisvesting (Case C-57/93) [1994]
    E.C.R. I–4541; 1 C.M.L.R. 881...................... 128

Wagner Miret v. Fondo de Garantia Salarial (Case 334/92) ECJ,
    Fifth Chamber [1993] E.C.R. I–6911; [1995] 2 C.M.L.R. 49 ... 10
Webb v. EMO Air Cargo (U.K.) Ltd (Case C-23/93) [1994] E.C.R.
    I–3567; [1992] C.M.L.R. 703 .... **10**, 11, **133**
Woodpulp. *See* Ahlstrom (A.) OY v. Commission (E.C.)
Worringham v. Lloyds Bank Ltd (Case 69/80) [1981] E.C.R. 767;
    [1981] 2 C.M.L.R. 1............................ **123**, 124
Wünsche Handelsgesellschaft, [1987] 3 C.M.L.R. 57............... 22

Zuckerfabrik Schoppenstedt v. Council (Case 5/71) E.C.R.
    975 .... 13, **46**, 47
Zuckerfabrik Suderdithmarschen AG v. Hauptzollamt Itzehoe
    (Case C-143/88) [1991] E.C.R. I–415; [1993] 3 C.M.L.R. 1... **58**

COMMISSION DECISIONS

A.C.E.C./Berliet, Re (Dec. 35/68) [1968] O.J. Spec. Ed.
    L201/7; [1968] C.M.L.R. D35 108
Prym/Beka, Re (Dec. 73/250) [1973] O.J. L296/24;
    [1973] C.M.L.R. D250 107
Vacuum Interrupters (No. 1), Re (Dec. 77/67) [1977] O.J.
    L48/32; [1977] 1 C.M.L.R. D67................. 107, 108
Unitel, Re (Dec. 78/516) [1978] O.J. L157/39; [1978]
    3 C.M.L.R. 306 99
Commission Decision (Dec. 85/381) [1985] O.J. L217/25.......... 19
ICI/Tioxide, Re (Case IV/M/023) [1990] O.J.
    C304/27; [1991] 4 C.M.L.R. M792.................. 118
Aerospatiale/Alexia/De Havilland, Re (Case IV/M/053)
    [1991] O.J. C280/122 [1992] 4 C.M.L.R. M2 119
Nestlé/Perrier, Re (Case IV/M/190) [1992] O.J.
    C80/10; [1993] 4 C.M.L.R. M17 119

TABLE OF ABBREVIATIONS

CAP	Common Agricultural Policy
CCT	Common Customs Tariff
CET	Common External Tariff
CFI	Court of First Instance
CMLR	Common Market Law Reports
E.C.	European Community/Communities
ECB	European Central Bank
ECJ	European Court of Justice
ECR	European Court Reports
ECSC	European Coal and Steel Community
ECU	European Currency Unit
EEA	European Economic Area
EEC	European Economic Community
EFTA	European Free Trade Association
EMU	European Monetary Union
E.P.	European Parliament
E.U.	European Union
EURATOM	European Atomic Energy Authority
IGC	Intergovernmental Conference
O.J.	Official Journal
SEA	Single European Act
TEU	Treaty on European Union

1. THE LEGAL ORDER OF THE E.C. AND E.U.

Introduction

The European Economic Community (EEC) was created in 1957 by the Treaty of Rome (EEC Treaty). The Treaty provided for a customs union and a common market (the free movement of goods, persons, services and capital) for the five signatory states (Germany, France, Italy, Belgium and Luxembourg). These states also created the European Coal and Steel Community (ECSC) and the European Atomic Energy Authority (Euratom). The United Kingdom, Denmark and Ireland joined in 1973. The United Kingdom enacted the European Communities Act (ECA 1972) in 1972 to give effect to its obligations under E.C. law. Further accessions took place in 1981 (Greece), 1986 (Spain and Portugal) and 1995 (Austria, Sweden and Finland).

There are four main institutions which serve the E.C., ECSC and Euratom: the Council of Ministers (an ad hoc body of ministers from the Member States responsible for the adoption of legislation); the Commission (a permanent body which proposes legislation and monitors the implementation of E.C. law); the European Parliament (E.P.) (directly elected since 1979 but with only a limited role in the legislative process) and the Court of Justice (the final authority on matters of E.C. law, now assisted by the Court of First Instance).

The EEC Treaty was amended in 1986 by the Single European Act (SEA) and in 1993 by the Treaty on European Union (TEU or the Maastricht Treaty), after which it was known as the E.C. Treaty. The SEA provided the mechanism to complete the single or internal market, an area without internal frontiers within which goods, persons, services and capital may circulate freely. The TEU created a three-pillar structure, namely:

[i] the E.C. (*i.e.* the ECSC, Euratom and the E.C., as the EEC was renamed);
[ii] the Common Foreign and Security Policy; and
[iii] Co-operation in Justice and Home Affairs.

The first pillar, the E.C., is governed by law under the E.C. Treaty, whereas the second and third pillars are administered through intergovernmental co-operation. The TEU provides for both political (EPU) and monetary union (EMU). The United Kingdom, through protocols annexed to the Treaty "opted out" of EMU and of the Agreement on Social Policy (usually known as the Social Chapter) which establishes a legal base for certain forms of employment protection.

The changes introduced by the TEU have been under review in an Intergovernmental Conference (IGC) from 1996 to 1997, leading to the finalisation of the Amsterdam Treaty in June 1997. Ratification is likely to take a considerable time. (The Maastricht Treaty took nearly two years from finalisation to ratification and involved various referenda and legal challenges.)

The Amsterdam Treaty will introduce into the Treaty an Employment Chapter, requiring Member States to co-ordinate their economic policies, focusing in growth and employment. While no change is made to the deadline for EMU (introduction of the single currency for participating states by 1999), inclusion of the Employment Chapter may be seen by some as a move away from the emphasis on strict economic criteria in EMU towards a recogniton of the social dimension.

The ECJ will have jurisdiction in certain areas relating to Co-operation in Justice and Home Affairs (the third pillar). The Social Chapter will be incorporated in the body of the revised Treaty, following the change of government in the United Kingdom. A Charter of Human Rights is provided, prohibiting discrimination on gender, race, religion, sexual orientation, or disability. Sanctions may be imposed on Member States for human rights' infringements.

The European Union (E.U.) will be given legal personality. The Schengen Agreement, by which participating states agreed to relax border formalities on the movement of people, was incorporated in the revised Treaty. The United Kingdom and Ireland have "opted out" of this part of the treaty; Denmark has obtained various exemptions.

The European leaders at Amsterdam were unable to agree on institutional reforms, a major issue which it had been hoped would be resolved before the admission of any new Member States. At least one year before membership of the E.U. exceeds twenty, an IGC will review the composition and functioning of the institutions. No changes have been made to the number of commissioners or the voting rights of Member States in the Council. Little progress was made on the principle of flexibility (intended to enable states to advance to European union at different rates).

The new legal order

KEY PRINCIPLE: *The objective of the E.C. is to establish a common market, the operation of which directly concerns interested parties in the Community.*

Van Gend en Loos v. Nederlandse Administratie der Belastinge (Case 26/62) 1963

Van Gend en Loos, a firm of importers, was required to pay customs duty on ureaformaldehyde (glue) imported from Germany into the Netherlands under a law adopted after the creation of the EEC. The importers challenged the payment in the Dutch courts on the basis that the extra duty infringed Article 12 of the EEC Treaty (prohibiting the introduction of new customs duties). The Dutch court referred questions to the Court of Justice (ECJ) for interpretation under Article 177 procedure.

HELD: (ECJ) (1) The EEC is a new legal order in international law, on behalf of which states have limited their sovereign rights in certain fields and whose subjects comprise not only states but also individuals; (2) Article 12 of the Treaty produces direct effects in the relationship between the Member States and their subjects, creating individual rights which national courts must protect. [1963] E.C.R. 1.

COMMENTARY
The "new legal order" is recognised in international law as a treaty between sovereign states but also takes effect within the domestic legal systems of the Member States. The order is characterised by the concepts of direct effect and the supremacy of E.C. law over national law. Where a provision of E.C. law is directly effective it creates rights and duties which are directly enforceable by individuals before the

national courts. The ECJ stated in *Van Gend en Loos* that to create direct effects a provision must be clear, unconditional and require no further action by Member States.

Supremacy and direct effect

KEY PRINCIPLE: *The EEC Treaty is an integral part of the legal system of the Member States and must be applied in their courts.*

Costa v. ENEL (Case 6/64) 1964

Ente Nazional Energia Elettrica (ENEL) was created by the Italian. Government under a law passed in 1962 to nationalise the electricity industry. Costa refused to pay his electricity bill, on the basis that the nationalisation infringed the Italian Constitution and various provisions of the Treaty.

HELD: (ECJ) The transfer by Member States from their domestic legal systems to the E.C. system of rights and duties carries with it a permanent limitation of their sovereign rights, against which a later, unilateral act incompatible with E.C. law cannot prevail. [1964] E.C.R. 585.

Italian Minister of Finance v. Simmenthal (Case 106/77) 1978

An Italian law introduced after joining the EEC required veterinary inspections of beef and veal. The law was challenged before the Italian courts as contrary to Article 30 (which prohibits quantitative restrictions on imports and measures having equivalent effect).

HELD: (ECJ) A national court in such circumstances should not apply conflicting national legislation, even in situations where it was adopted after joining the EEC; it should not wait for the decision of a higher national court before acting. [1978] E.C.R. 629.

COMMENTARY
(1) Article 177 enables the ECJ to interpret or consider the validity of E.C. law (see Chapter 7). The ECJ has used this procedure to develop the concept of the new legal order and to provide authoritative rulings which apply uniformly throughout all the Member States. (2) The United Kingdom recog-

nised the direct effect of E.C. law in section 2(1) of the European Communities Act 1972.

Interim relief

KEY PRINCIPLE: *The full effectiveness of E.C. law would be impaired if a rule of national law could prevent a court considering a matter governed by E.C. law from granting interim relief.*

R. v. Secretary of State for Transport, ex p. Factortame (Case C-213/89) 1990

Following concern about the tenuous nature of the link between the owners of a number of fishing vessels and the United Kingdom the Merchant Shipping Act 1988 was adopted, setting out stringent rules for the registration of fishing vessels as British. Many vessels owned by Spanish nationals previously registered as British no longer qualified and thus could not share in the United Kingdom fishing quota under the common fisheries policy. The unsuccessful applicants sought judicial review in the United Kingdom and suspension of the relevant parts of the 1988 Act, arguing that the Act contravened various provisions of the Treaty. An injunction against the Secretary of State was refused. The House of Lords referred questions for interpretation to the ECJ under Article 177.

HELD: (ECJ) A national law should be set aside where it prevents the granting of interim relief in a dispute governed by E.C. law. [1990] E.C.R. I–2433.

COMMENTARY
The ruling of the ECJ followed the interim decision of the same court in an enforcement action brought by the Commission against the United Kingdom under Article 169: *Commission v. U.K.* (Case–246/89 R), ordering the United Kingdom to suspend the operation of the offending sections of the 1988 Act. The House of Lords applied the decision and set aside the rule that an interim injunction cannot be granted against the Crown in *R. v. Secretary of State for Transport, ex p. Factortame* (1991). The ECJ later ruled on the interpretation of the substantive provisions of the Treaty (in Case C-221/89R),

holding that Articles 52, etc., were infringed in circumstances where registration was made more difficult for nationals from other Member States than for nationals from the host state.

The direct effect of regulations, directives and decisions

KEY PRINCIPLE: *Regulations, directives and decisions are capable of creating direct effects.*

Grad v. Finanzamt Traunstein (Case 9/70) 1970

A haulage contractor challenged a German transport tax on the basis that it infringed a decision addressed to the Member States on VAT and a harmonisation directive imposing a deadline for implementation of the decision.

HELD: (ECJ) (1) The wording of Article 189 does not prevent individuals from relying in the national courts on decisions addressed to Member States. (2) The decision was directly effective; the directive merely fixed the date on which the VAT regime in the decision took effect. [1970] E.C.R. 825.

COMMENTARY
The ECJ adopted the same reasoning in *Van Duyn v. Home Office* (Case 41/74), holding that directives can be directly effective. Regulations are stated in Article 189 to be "of general application". If they are also clear and unconditional, they may be directly effective: *Leonesio v. Italian Minister of Agriculture* (Case 93/71).

KEY PRINCIPLE: *A directive containing a deadline for implementation is only capable of creating direct effects from the date of the deadline.*

Pubblico Ministero v. Ratti (Case 148/78) 1979

Ratti, a manufacturer of solvents in Italy, was charged with failure to comply with Italian labelling legislation. He claimed that his products were labelled according to E.C. standards contained in two directives.

HELD: (ECJ) As the deadline for implementation had been reached in relation to one but not both of the directives, only the directive for which the deadline had expired could be relied upon to create direct effects (and thus to provide a defence to one of the criminal charges). [1972] E.C.R. 119.

COMMENTARY
If no deadline is specified in a directive it takes effect on publication in the Official Journal.

Vertical and horizontal direct effects

KEY PRINCIPLE: *Treaty provisions are capable of creating direct effects both vertically between the state and individuals and horizontally between individuals.*

Defrenne v. Sabena (Case 43/75) 1976
Ms D, an airline stewardess employed by the Belgian airline Sabena, was paid less and had to retire earlier than male stewards. She claimed that this amounted to a breach of Article 119 of the Treaty (which provides for equal pay for equal work).

HELD: (concerning Article 177) Article 119 creates direct effects both vertically and horizontally. [1976] E.C.R. 4545.

COMMENTARY
The ruling in *Defrenne* was limited to Treaty provisions. Article 119 was treated as directly effective only from the date of the judgment. This ruling on temporal effect was unusual but not unique and was based on the need for legal certainty. See also *Barber v. Guardian Royal Exchange* (Case C-262/88) (Chapter 13, p. 125).

KEY PRINCIPLE: *Directives are capable of creating direct effects vertically but not horizontally.*

Marshall v. South West Area Health Authority (No. 1) (Case 152/84) 1986
Ms M sought to rely on Article 5 of the Equal Treatment Directive 76/207 when she was required to retire at 60 when

men did not have to retire until the age of 65. The House of Lords referred questions to the ECJ.

HELD: (ECJ) (1) Differentiating between retirement ages for men and women contravenes Article 5 of the Directive. (2) The obligation in a directive is addressed to Member States and cannot be enforced against individuals. (3) As an area health authority is a public body, the obligation not to discriminate may be enforced directly against that body. [1986] E.C.R. 723.

COMMENTARY
(1) *Marshall* established for the first time that directives cannot be enforced directly against individuals, unless the individual is a public body (or "emanation of the state"). (2) In *Foster v. British Gas* (Case C-188/89) the ECJ held that a directive could be enforced against a body responsible for providing a public service under state control, possessing special powers greater than those normally applicable between individuals (*e.g.* privatised utilities such as gas, water and electricity). (3) The limitation on the direct effect of directives was upheld in *Faccini Dori v. Recreb* (Case C–91/92). (Ms F.D. could not rely on the cooling-off period in a consumer protection directive against an Italian company when she sought to cancel a contract for a language course entered into on Milan Station.) (4) The lack of horizontal direct effect in directives was again confirmed in *El Corte Ingles SA v. Rivero* (Case–C192/94). In this case it was held that Article 129a E.C. (providing that the E.C. shall contribute to the attainment of a high level of consumer protection) cannot justify the direct effect of a directive on consumer protection which has not been transposed into national law.

Indirect effect

KEY PRINCIPLE: *Where a directive is indirectly effective (i.e. not directly effective) national legislation must be interpreted in the light of the wording and purpose of the directive.*

Von Colson and Kamann v. Land Nordhein-Westfalen (Case 14/83) 1984
Ms Von Colson and Ms Kamann had applied for posts as social workers in a German prison. The officials responsible for recruitment refused to appoint the two women, although they

had been placed at the top of the list of applicants by the social work committee, because of the problems and risks associated with working in a male prison. They claimed that they should be granted a contract of employment or damages under Article 6 of Directive 76/207. The German courts made an Article 177 reference.

HELD: (ECJ) (1) Article 6 of Directive 76/207 does not satisfy the requirements for creating direct effects. (2) The duty of Member States to achieve the results envisaged by the directive and their duty under Article 5 to ensure fulfilment of that obligation binds all authorities within the Member States including the courts. National courts must interpret and apply legislation adopted to implement a directive in the light of the wording and purpose of the directive in order to achieve the objective of the directive. [1986] E.C.R. 1891.

COMMENTARY
(1) Rather than treating the question as one concerned with the supremacy of E.C. law over national law, the ECJ developed a rule of construction in *Von Colson* derived from Article 189 (Directive binding on Member State to whom addressed, with choice of form and method left to the national authorities) and Article 5 (Member States must take all appropriate measures to ensure fulfilment of the obligations arising from the Treaty or secondary legislation).
(2) In *Kolpinghuis Nijmegen* (Case 80/86) the ECJ repeated the formula in *Von Colson* but added that a directive cannot independently create criminal liability where its provisions are infringed.
(3) United Kingdom law provides for the implementation of indirectly effective E.C. law in section 2(2) of the ECA 1972.

KEY PRINCIPLE: *The obligation to interpret national law to comply with a directive applies regardless of whether the national law was adopted before or after the directive.*

Marleasing S.A. v. La Commercial Internacional de Alimtacion S.A. (Case C-106/89) 1990

Marleasing S.A. had sued La Commercial and several other companies in the Spanish courts. M claimed that the defendant companies had been established by Barviesa, who owed M large sums of money, in order to put his assets beyond the reach of his creditors. M sought a declaration that the contract establishing the companies was void for lack of cause under the Spanish Civil Code. La Commercial claimed that the action should be dismissed because lack of cause was not listed in Article 11 of Directive 68/151 which listed nullity grounds exhaustively. An Article 177 reference was made.

HELD: (ECJ) In applying national law, whether the provisions in question were adopted before or after the Directive, the national court must interpret it, as far as possible, in the light of the wording and purpose of the directive in order to achieve the result pursued by the directive and to comply with Article 189(3). [1990] E.C.R. I-4135.

COMMENTARY
(1) It followed from the ruling in *Marleasing* that the Spanish Civil Code had to be interpreted in line with the directive, thus excluding lack of cause as a ground for annulment of the contract.
(2) The obligation to interpret national law to conform with an E.C. obligation is stated to apply "as far as possible".
(3) In *Wagner Miret v. Fondo de Garantia Salarial* (Case C-334/92) the ECJ accepted that it was impossible to interpret pre-existing legislation so as to comply with Directive 80/987 on the protection of employees in the event of their employer's insolvency. In such circumstances the state may be obliged to compensate the applicant for his loss under the *Francovich* principle (see p. 11).

KEY PRINCIPLE: *It is for the national courts to decide in each case whether it is possible to interpret national law to accord with a directive or whether it would distort the meaning of the national law.*

Webb v. EMO Air Cargo (U.K.) Ltd. 1992

Ms Webb was engaged by EMO for an indefinite term while another employee was on maternity leave. She was dismissed when she found that she, too, was pregnant. The House of Lords had to consider whether EMO was entitled to dismiss Ms Webb. This required the court to decide whether it could construe the Sex Discrimination Act 1975 in accord with the Equal Treatment Directive 76/207. The House of Lords referred questions to the ECJ.

HELD: (H.L.) It is for the United Kingdom court to construe domestic legislation in any field covered by an E.C. directive so as to accord with the interpretation of the directive as laid down by the ECJ, if that can be done without distorting the meaning of the domestic legislation.

COMMENTARY
(1) The ECJ ruled that it was a breach of Directive 76/207 to dismiss a female employee who was pregnant who had been recruited for an unlimited term, even if she had been engaged as a maternity leave replacement (see Chapter 13, p. 133). The House of Lords applied the ruling and interpreted the United Kingdom law in accordance with the directive.
(2) *Webb v. EMO* represents a clear statement by the House of Lords of the duty of the United Kingdom courts to give effect to E.C. law when interpreting national law. *Webb* was decided after *Marleasing* and should be contrasted with its earlier decision in *Duke v. Reliance Systems* (H.L. 1988) in which it had held that it would distort the meaning of the Sex Discrimination Act 1975 to interpret it so as to give effect to Directive 76/207.

State liability for breach of E.C. law

KEY PRINCIPLE: *A Member State will be liable for non–implementation of a directive in certain circumstances.*

Francovich, Bonifaci and others v. Italy (Cases C-6 & 9/90) 1991

Italy had failed to implement Directive 80/987 on the protection of workers in the event of insolvency. (The Directive required the guarantee of payments of oustanding claims for remuneration and the creation of guarantee institutions to meet those claims.) Italy's breach was establised by the ECJ in *Commission v. Italy* (Case 22/87). Francovich and Bonifaci had outstanding claims against a company declared bankrupt in 1985. Unable to recover against the company they brought actions in the Italian courts against Italy, requesting that Italy should pay them compensation in the light of the obligation in the directive. Both national courts referred questions to the ECJ to determine the extent of a Member State's liability.

HELD: (ECJ) Member States are obliged to compensate individuals for breaches of E.C. law for which they are responsible if three conditions are satisfied:
(1) The objective of the directive must include the conferring of rights for the benefit of individuals.
(2) The content of the rights must be identifiable from the directive.
(3) There must be a causal link between the breach and the damage. [1991] E.C.R. I-5357.

COMMENTARY

(1) The ECJ in *Francovich* stated that the full effectiveness of E.C. law would be impaired if individuals were unable to obtain compensation when their rights were infringed by a breach attributable to a Member State. The principle of state liability is inherent in the scheme of the Treaty. The duty on Member States to compensate derives from Article 5 which obliges them to ensure fulfilment of their obligations under E.C. law.
(2) State liability under *Francovich* applies to obligations which may not be directly effective and provides a remedy in the event of non-implementation (or inadequate implementation) of E.C. law. Thus it prevents a state from relying on its own default in implementing E.C. law.
(3) The ruling has been of immense importance and has led to a number of later rulings clarifying and extending the principle.

KEY PRINCIPLE: *States are liable for breaches of E.C. law where the breach is sufficiently serious.*

Brasserie du Pêcheur S.A. v. Germany (Case C-46/93) and R. v. Secretary of State for Transport, ex p. Factortame Ltd (No. 3) (Case C-48/93) 1996

These cases both concerned the question of the extent of state liability where legislation had been adopted in contravention of directly effective rights. *Brasserie du Pêcheur* arose out of a claim by a French brewery against Germany for losses incurred as a result of the German Beer Purity laws which had been found by the ECJ to infringe Article 30 (Case 178/84). *Factortame* (see p. 5) had led to a finding that the Merchant Shipping Act 1988 infringed E.C. law. The Spanish trawler owners claimed compensation from the United Kingdom courts. An Article 177 reference was made to the ECJ.

HELD: (ECJ) Where a Member State acts in a field where it has a wide discretion, it will be liable to an individual for breach of E.C. law provided:
(1) the rule of law infringed is intended to confer rights on indviduals;
(2) the breach is sufficiently serious;
(3) there is a direct causal link between the breach and the damage. [1996] 1 C.M.L.R. 889.

COMMENTARY
(1) The first and third conditions correspond to *Francovich*. However, the position of the Member States was compared with that of the E.C. institutions under Article 215 (see chapter 6, p. 44). The E.C. institutions are liable in relation to legislative measures involving choices of economic policy where the breach is "sufficiently serious", *i.e.* when it is "manifest and grave" under the *Schoppenstedt* formula: see chapter 6, p. 46.
(2) It was held that reparation may not be made conditional on fault or on a prior finding by the ECJ and that the amount must be commensurate with the damage sustained. No temporal restriction was placed on the effect of the judgment.
(3) The German Federal Court applied the ruling of the ECJ in *Brasserie du Pêcheur v. Germany* in 1996. It held that there was no direct causal link between the breach of Article 30 and the applicant's loss. It also found that the infringement in relation to additives was not sufficiently serious. The brewer's claim against the German Government thus failed.
(4) The United Kingdom Divisional Court in *Factortame (No. 5)* held in 1997 that the trawler owners were entitled to damages, but not to punitive damages.

KEY PRINCIPLE: *Incorrect implementation of an imprecisely worded directive does not necessarily give rise to state liability.*

R. v. H.M. Treasury, ex p. British Telecommunications plc (Case C-392/93) 1996

BT claimed that the United Kingdom had incorrectly implemented Directive 90/531 covering the procurement (purchasing) procedures of bodies contracting in the telecommunications sector (*e.g.* BT and Mercury). In particular, BT alleged that the procedures adopted by the United Kingdom for exemption had put BT at a competitive disadvantage. The United Kingdom court referred questions to the ECJ.

HELD: (ECJ) The three conditions in *Brasserie du Pêcheur/ Factortame* must be satisfied. However, when transposing the directive into national law, the United Kingdom Government had not gravely and manifestly disregarded the limits on the exercise of their power. The breach was not sufficiently serious to impose liability. [1996] All E.R. (E.C.) 411.

COMMENTARY

The ECJ appears to have accepted that the breach was not sufficiently serious because the obligation in the directive was imprecisely worded and could reasonably have borne the interpretation placed on it by the United Kingdom Government. No guidance had been provided to the United Kingdom by the ECJ and the Commission had not objected to the United Kingdom's implementing regulations.

KEY PRINCIPLE: *The mere fact of infringement of E.C. law may be enough to establish the existence of a sufficiently serious breach.*

R. v. Minister of Agriculture, Fisheries and Food, ex p. Hedley Lomas (Ireland) Ltd. (Case C–5/94) 1996

MAFF refused to grant licences to enable Hedley Lomas to export live sheep to Spain because it considered that Spain had not implemented properly an E.C. directive dealing with the pre–slaughter condition of certain animals. The Commission investigated but found no breach by Spain. It informed the United Kingdom that its export ban infringed Article 34 and was not justified under Article 36. When proceedings were brought in the United Kingdom courts an Article 177 reference was made.

HELD: (ECJ) (1) Recourse to Article 36 is impossible where harmonisation has occurred.

(2) A Member State may not act unilaterally to avoid a breach of E.C. law by another Member State.

(3) Where a Member State does not have to make legislative choices or has only reduced discretion, the mere fact of infringement of E.C. law may be enough to establish a sufficiently serious breach.

(4) It is for the national court to determine whether there is a causal link between duty and the damage.

(5) If state liability is established, the state must make good any loss in accordance with its domestic law on liability. [1996] All E.R. (E.C.) 493.

COMMENTARY
See also *Dillenkofer v. Federal Republic of Germany* (Joined Cases C-178 etc./94): intentional fault is not an essential pre-condition to state liability.

---

2. THE INSTITUTIONS OF THE E.C. AND E.U.

The European Parliament

KEY PRINCIPLE: *Failure to consult the E.P., where required by the Treaty, is a breach of an essential procedural requirement.*

Roquette Frères v. Council (Case 138/79) 1980

The Council adopted a regulation before it had received the opinion of the E.P. under Article 40(3). It was challenged by a producer affected by the measure. (See Chapter 5, p. 41.)

HELD: (ECJ) Consultation under Article 43(3) is the means whereby the E.P. participates in the legislative process of the

E.C. Failure to consult was a breach of an essential procedural requirement, as a result of which the measure concerned was void. [1980] E.C.R. 3393.

COMMENTARY
The ECJ stated in *Roquette Frères* that consultation "reflects at Community level the fundamental democratic principle that the peoples should take part in the exercise of power through the intermediary of an intermediate assembly".

KEY PRINCIPLE: *The E.P. may take action in the ECJ to protect its prerogative.*

E.P. v. Council (Re Students' Rights) (Case C-295/90)

The Commission proposed a directive on residence rights for students undertaking vocational courses based on Article 7(2) of the Treaty (under the co-operation procedure requiring qualified majority voting). After the E.P.'s opinion had been received the draft was submitted to the Council which amended the legal basis to Article 235 (general power requiring unanimity).

HELD: (ECJ) The E.P. may bring actions to safeguard its prerogatives. [1992] 3 C.M.L.R. 281.

COMMENTARY
Although the E.P. had not expressly mentioned Article 173, the fact that the Council's action deprived the E.P. of a second reading was enough to justify a challenge. This right is expressly provided in the revised wording of Article 173, following amendment by the TEU. (See Chapter 5 p. 37.)

KEY PRINCIPLE: *If the Council or Commission fails to act, in infringement of the Treaty, the E.P. may bring an action in the ECJ: Article 175.*

E.P. v. Council (Case 13/83) 1985

The E.P. sought a declaration that the Council had infringed the EEC Treaty by failing to adopt a Common Transport Policy. The Council objected, claiming that the E.P. lacked competence to bring an action under Article 175.

HELD: (ECJ) The E.P. had capacity to bring an action under Article 175 and had observed the conditions of that provision in bringing the action. The action was upheld in part, but rejected where the obligation was too vague to be enforceable. (See Chapter 5, p. 42.)

The Council of the European Union

KEY PRINCIPLE: *Regulations, directives and decisions adopted jointly by the E.P. and the Council, and such acts adopted by the Council or Commission, shall state the reasons on which they are based and shall refer to any proposals or opinions which were required to be obtained under the Treaty: Article 190.*

KEY PRINCIPLE: *If action by the E.C. is necessary, in the course of the operation of the common market, to attain one of the objectives of the E.C. and the Treaty has not provided the necessary powers, the Council shall take the appropriate measures acting on a proposal from the Commission and after consulting the E.P.*

Commission v. Council (Case 45/86) 1987

The Commission brought annulment proceedings under Article 173 (see Chapter 5) against two regulations adopted by the Council relating to generalised tariff preferences for products from developing countries. The Commission claimed that there was no explicit legal basis stated in the measures. The Council argued that it had intended to base the measures on both Articles 113 (the Common Commercial Policy) and 235.

HELD: (ECJ) It follows from the wording of Article 235 that its use as the legal basis for a measure is justified only where no other provision of the treaty gives the E.C. institutions the necessary power to adopt the measure in question. As Article 113 would have provided an appropriate legal basis, the Council was not justified in relying on Article 235. [1987] E.C.R. 1493.

COMMENTARY
(1) The choice of legal basis determines the procedure which is followed in the adoption of the measure. Article 235, unlike

Article 113, requires unanimity in the Council, thus making it possible for individual states to veto a proposed measure. (2) As a result of the TEU amendments the Council has become known as the Council of the E.U., with responsibility extending beyond the area of legal control under the E.C. Treaty to the areas of political co-operation (the Common Foreign and Security Policy, and Justice and Home Affairs). The other institutions remain institutions of the E.C.

KEY PRINCIPLE: *The Council, acting by qualified majority on a proposal from the Commission, in co-operation with the E.P. and after consulting the Economic and Social Committee, shall adopt measures which have as their object the establishment and functioning of the internal market: Article 100A EC Treaty.*

Commission v. Council (Case C-300/89) 1991

The Commission brought annulment proceedings under Article 173 against the Council in relation to a directive harmonising programmes to eliminate pollution caused by waste from the titanium dioxide industry. The directive in question had been based on Article 130S which (following the consultation procedure under the EEC Treaty prior to amendment by the TEU) enabled the Council to adopt measures relating to environment protection by unanimity, on a proposal from the Commission, after consulting the E.P. and the Economic and Social Committee. The Commission claimed that the measure should have been adopted under Article 100A (the co-operation procedure, requiring qualified majority voting and two consultations with the E.P.) as a single market measure.

HELD: (ECJ) (1) The choice of legal basis must be based on objective factors which are amenable to judicial review. (2) The measure should have been based on Article 100A, not Article 130S. [1991] E.C.R. I-2867.

COMMENTARY
(1) While the Directive displayed features relating both to the environment and to the establishment and functioning of the internal market, recourse to a dual basis was excluded by the ECJ. An E.C. measure cannot be treated as an environmental

measure merely because it pursues objectives of environmental protection. Action to harmonise national rules on
industrial production with a view to eliminating distortion of
competition is covered by Article 100A.
(2) This case was considered under the EEC Treaty. After
amendment by the TEU, the procedure governing the adoption of internal market rules under Article 100A is the co-
decision procedure (Article 189B), by which the E.P. is jointly
responsible for the adoption of legislation and which provides
for more extensive consultation with the E.P. Environmental
measures under Article 130S now adopted under the consultation procedure set out in Article 189C.

The Commission

KEY PRINCIPLE: *The Commission shall have the task of
promoting close co-operation between Member States in the
social field. To this end the Commission shall act in close
contact with Member States by making studies, delivering
opinions and arranging consultations both on problems arising at national level and on those of concern to international
organisations: Article 118.*

Germany, France, Netherlands, Denmark and the United Kingdom v. Commission (Joined Cases 281, 283 and 287/85) 1987

Germany and the other applicant states sought annulment
under Article 173 of Decision 85/381 in relation to the migra-
tion policy of non-member countries. The challenge was
brought on the grounds that such a policy was outside the
social field and that the arrangement of consultation under
Article 118 did not empower the Commission to adopt binding
measures.

HELD: (ECJ) (1) The promotion of the integration into the
workforce of non-member countries must be held to be within
the social field within the meaning of Article 118, in so far as it
is linked to employment.
(2) The promotion of cultural integration goes beyond the

social field but may be justified under Article 118(2) (power to arrange consultations). [1987] E.C.R. 3203.

COMMENTARY

(1) Where the Treaty confers a specific task on the Commission, it also confers on it the powers which are indispensible to carry out the task, in this case to carry out the consultations. It follows that where the institutions have competence, the Member States have restricted their own powers.

(2) This case provides an example of the exercise of implied powers. See also *E.P. v. Council (re Erta)* (Case 13/83) above.

KEY PRINCIPLE: *The public shall have access to measures adopted by the Council unless the release of such documents would undermine the protection of the public interest, individual privacy, commercial and industrial secrecy, the E.C.'s financial interests or confidentiality requested by natural or legal persons: Article 1 of Decision 93/731 (adopted pursuant to an Appendix to the TEU containing a declaration on public access to information from E.C.).*

Carvel & Guardian Newspapers v. Council (Case T-194/94) 1995

Carvel, the European Affairs Editor of the Guardian, requested various documents relating to meetings of the Social Affairs and Justice Council in 1993 and the Agriculture Committee in 1994. The Council's Secretariat refused, stating that the documents related directly to the deliberations of the Council and could not be disclosed. The applicants challenged the decision under Article 173.

HELD: (CFI) Decision 93/731 requires the balancing of the applicants' interests in gaining access with the Council's interests in maintaining confidentiality. By automatically refusing access to the documents the Council had failed to exercise discretion in accordance with the decision. [1995] 3 C.M.L.R. 359.

COMMENTARY

After the ruling of the CFI the Council agreed to facilitate the release of minutes of meetings, to broadcast debates on matters of public interest and to release details of votes on legislative acts. Carvel remains dissatisfied and is pursuing a further action against the Council.

3. FUNDAMENTAL RIGHTS AND GENERAL PRINCIPLES

KEY PRINCIPLE: *Fundamental rights and the general principles of E.C. law are protected by the ECJ.*

Stauder v. City of Ulm (Case 29/69) 1969

A Commission regulation provided for the recipients of welfare benefits to receive free butter. When the scheme was implemented the German Government required beneficiaries to produce a coupon bearing their name and address. S claimed that the German decision implementing the scheme infringed the general principles of E.C. law. An Article 177 reference was made to the ECJ by the German administrative court.

HELD: (ECJ) The provision in issue contained nothing capable of prejudicing the fundamental human rights enshrined in the general principles of E.C. law and protected by the Court. [1969] E.C.R. 419.

COMMENTARY
(1) The tentative statement in *Stauder* is the first acknowledgement by the ECJ that fundamental rights are recognised by E.C. law. In its subsequent case law the ECJ has developed its approach to fundamental rights, providing a mechanism to review that validity of action by the E.C. institutions and by the Member States. Fundamental rights and general principles are most often invoked in annulment proceedings under Article 173 (see Chapter 5), to claim damages under Article 215 (see Chapter 6) and as a guide to the interpretation of E.C. law (see Chapter 1).
(2) General principles derive from: (a) international law, *e.g.* the European Convention of Human Rights, (b) principles which are accepted by the domestic legal systems of the Member States and (c) the decisions of the ECJ.

KEY PRINCIPLE: *Respect for fundamental rights forms an integral part of the general principles of law protected by the ECJ.*

Internationale Handelsgesellschaft mbH v. Einfuhr-und Vorratsstelle für Getreide und Futtermittel (Case 11/70) 1970

The applicants had obtained a licence to export maize from Germany, conditional under an E.C. regulation on lodging a deposit which acted as a guarantee that the exportation would be carried out while the licence was valid. As the exportation was not completed during the validity of the licence, the German administrative authorities ordered the forfeiture of a large part of the deposit. The applicants challenged the forfeiture on the basis that it contravened certain principles of German law in the Frankfurt administrative court which made an Article 177 reference to the ECJ.

HELD: (ECJ) (1) The validity of a measure of E.C. law cannot be affected by allegations that it contravenes national fundamental rights or national constitutional principles.
(2) The protection of fundamental rights, while inspired by the constitutional traditions common to the Member States, must be ensured within the framework and structure of the objectives of the E.C. [1970] E.C.R. 1125.

COMMENTARY
(1) See also *Nold v. Commission* (Case 4/73) in which the ECJ declared that it would not uphold measures which are incompatible with fundamental rights recognised and protected by the constitutions of the Member States. (2) In the early years the German Constitutional Court did not accept the supremacy of E.C. law on fundamental rights expressed in decisions such as *Handelsgesellschaft*. This view was modifed in *Wünsche Handelsgesellschaft* (1987) where the German court accepted that the protection of fundamental rights under E.C. law had reached the level of German law. However, in *Brunner v. E.U. Treaty* (1994) the Constitutional Court reasserted its right to review the legitimacy of E.C. law (see Chapter 1).

Legal certainty

Non-retroactivity

KEY PRINCIPLE: *Penal provisions may not take effect retro-actively.*

R. v. Kirk (Case 63/83) 1984

Captain Kirk, a Danish fisherman, was charged with fishing in the United Kingdom's 12 mile coastal fishing zone, contrary to United Kingdom law. Although the United Kingdom was entitled under the Act of Accession to exclude non-United Kingdom fishing vessels from the 12 mile zone until December 31, 1982, Captain Kirk had been fishing on January 6, 1983. The E.C. subsequently adopted a regulation permitting the United Kingdom to maintain the exclusion for a further 10 years, backdated to January 1, 1983. The United Kingdom court made an Article 177 reference. [1984] E.C.R. 2689.

HELD: (ECJ) Non-retroactivity of penal provisions is common to all the Member States and enshrined in Article 7 of the ECHR. It is one of the general principles of E.C. law.

COMMENTARY
The ECJ has upheld a number of individual provisions of the ECHR as general principles of E.C. law: see *e.g. National Panasonic (U.K.) Ltd. v. Commission* (Case 136/79): Article 8 (right to privacy); *VBVB v. Commission* (Cases 43 & 63/82): Article 10 (right to expression). While the E.C. is not a party to the ECHR it has recognised the importance of fundamental rights in Article F(2) of the TEU: the Union shall respect fundamental rights, as guaranteed by the ECHR and as they result from the constitutional traditions common to the Member States, as general principles of E.C. law. (This provision is outside the E.C. Treaty and so non-justiciable in the ECJ.)

Legitimate expectations

KEY PRINCIPLE: *E.C. measures must not infringe the legitimate expectations of those concerned in the absence of overriding public interest.*

Mulder v. Minister van Landbouw en Visserig (Case 120/86) 1988

Mulder and other milk producers decided not to deliver milk for five years under an E.C. scheme to reduce an excess supply of milk. After that time they were unable to resume deliveries because provision under an E.C. regulation was based on a reference year during the five years of non-delivery.

HELD: (ECJ) Where a producer has been encouraged by an E.C. provision to suspend marketing in the general interest and against the payment of a premium he may legitimately expect not to be subjected to restrictions because he has acted on the provision. [1988] E.C.R. 2321.

COMMENTARY

An expectation is only legitimate where it is reasonable rather than speculative. Challenges to E.C. legislation based on a breach of legitimate expectations rarely succeed.

Proportionality

KEY PRINCIPLE: *Measures should not exceed what is appropriate and necessary to achieve the objectives in question.*

R. v. Intervention Board for Agricultural Produce, ex p. Man (Sugar) (Case 181/84) 1986

As a result of applying for an export licence four hours late the Commission ruled that the entire deposit was forfeit under the terms of a regulation. The Divisional Court in the United Kingdom made an Article 177 reference.

HELD: (ECJ) The forfeiture of the entire deposit was a disproportionate penalty for a minor breach. The regulation was annulled to the extent that it required the forfeiture. [1985] E.C.R. 2889.

COMMENTARY

(1) Proportionality, like a number of other general principles, derives from German law, although there are some similarities with reasonableness in English law. Proportionality oper-

ates by weighing the objectives of legislation against the means by which they are achieved. The principle operates to restrain public authorities from imposing unnecessarily restrictive measures. (2) Proportionality is frequently invoked in the context of single market measures. Under the *Cassis de Dijon* principle (see Chapter 8, p. 64) restrictions on imports may be permissible if necessary to justify a mandatory requirement provided they are not disproportionate. (In *Cassis* (Case-120/78) it was disproportionate to ban the sale of drinks below a certain alcohol level. Labelling would have provided the customer with sufficient information.) Proportionality is incorporated in the principle of subsidiarity under Article 3b (see p. 27 below).

Equality

KEY PRINCIPLE: *Persons in similar situations should be treated alike unless differential treatment is objectively justified.*

Sabbatini v. E.P. (Case 20/71) 1972

Mrs Sabbatini sought the annulment of decisions whereby the expatriation allowance she had previously received from the E.P. was withdrawn following her marriage. The allowance was payable to the "head of the family", normally considered to be the husband except in cases of serious illnes or invalidity.

HELD: (ECJ) Determination of the status of expatriate must be dependent on uniform criteria, irrespective of sex. The decisions taken with regard to the applicant were annulled. [1972] E.C.R. 345.

COMMENTARY
The E.C. Treaty recognises the principle of equality (or non–discrimination) on grounds of nationality (Article 6 E.C., formerly Article 7 EEC), sex (Article 119: equal pay for equal work) and against producers or consumers under the CAP (Article 40(3)). Equality of treatment has been extended by secondary legislation into such areas as access to employment and housing (Directive 76/207). Equality of treatment is essential to secure the free movement of goods, persons, services and capital (*e.g.* Article 36: exception to the free

movement of goods, provided there is no discrimination on grounds of nationality. See Chapter 8.). The ECJ has applied the principle imaginatively to meet the demands of the single market. See *e.g. Cowan v. Tresor Public* (Case 186/87): Chapter 11, p. 96.

Procedural rights

Right to a hearing

KEY PRINCIPLE: *A person whose interests are affected by a decision must be given the opportunity to be heard.*

Transocean Marine Paints Association v. Commission (Case 17/74) 1974

The Commission reached a competition decision concerning exemption under Article 85(3) of an agreement between the undertakings making up the Association without hearing the Association's observations. The Association challenged the decision under Article 173.

HELD: (ECJ) Interested parties have a right to be heard. The offending part of the decision was annulled (see Chapter 5, p. 41). [1974] E.C.R. 1063.

Right to effective judicial control

KEY PRINCIPLE: *The individual is entitled to effective judicial control.*

Johnston v. Chief Constable of the Royal Ulster Constabulary (Case 222/84) 1986

Mrs Johnston, a member of the full-time Reserve of the Royal Ulster Constabulary (RUC), brought an action before an industrial tribunal challenging the decision of the Chief Constable of the RUC not to renew her contract and to refuse her training in firearms. The Chief Constable had decided, in the light of the large number of police officers killed in Northern Ireland, that male police officers would carry firearms in future. Women would not be equipped with firearms and would not receive firearms training. In the industrial tribunal the Chief Constable produced a certificate issued by the Secretary of State for Northern Ireland, stating that Mrs Johnston's contract had not been renewed in order to safeguard national security and to protect public safety and public order. Under Article 53 of the Northern Ireland Order the certificate was considered to be "conclusive evidence of purpose". Mrs Johnston claimed that the action contravened Article 6 of Directive 76/207 (obligation on Member States to introduce measures to enable applicants to pursue equal treatment claims before the courts). (See Chapter 14, p. 135).

HELD: (ECJ) The principle of judicial control in Article 6 of Directive 76/207 reflects Articles 6 and 13 of the ECHR. It entitles all persons to an effective remedy in a competent court against measures which they consider contrary to the principle of equal treatment for men and women. The national courts must interpret a provision such as Article 53 of the Northern Ireland Order in the light of Directive 76/207.

COMMENTARY
Other procedural rights which have been recognised by the ECJ include the duty to give reasons: *UNECTEF v. Heylens* (Case 222/86); and the right to protection against self-incrimination: *Orkem v. Commission* (Case 374/87) and *Solvay v. Commission* (Case 27/88) (in the context of criminal proceedings only, and therefore not applicable to the competition investigations in question).

Subsidiarity

KEY PRINCIPLE: *The E.C. must act within the limits of the powers conferred on it by the Treaty. In areas outside the E.C.'s exclusive competence, the E.C. must act in accordance with the principle of subsidiarity only if the proposed action cannot be sufficiently achieved by the Member States.*

U.K. v. Council (The Working Time Directive) (Case C-84/94) 1996
The Council adopted Directive 93/104 based on Article 118a of the E.C. Treaty (harmonisation of health and safety in the working environment), providing, *inter alia*, that average weekly

working time should not exceed 48 hours, that there should be specified minimum rest periods and that workers should be entitled to four weeks' annual paid leave. The United Kingdom challenged the measure under Article 173, claiming that it should have been adopted under Article 100 (requiring a unanimous vote) rather than Article 118a (qualified majority vote), and that it contravened the principle of subsidiarity.

HELD: (ECJ) (1) The measure was properly adopted under Article 118a (except for the second sentence of Article 5, specifying Sunday for a rest day: annulled).
(2) The adoption of the directive was not inconsistent with the principle of subsidiarity. [1996] 3 C.M.L.R. 671.

COMMENTARY
(1) Subsidiarity was introduced into the E.C. Treaty by the TEU. It represents a check on the powers of the E.C. institutions by creating a presumption in favour of action by the Member States in areas where the E.C. does not possess exclusive powers (*e.g.* competition policy, environmental protection, education, transport). Article 3b of the Treaty incorporates the principle of proportionality by stating that action by the E.C. shall not exceed what is necessary to achieve the objectives of the Treaty.
(2) In *U.K. v. Council* the need to improve the existing level of health and safety of workers through the imposition of minimum requirements presupposed E.C.-wide action. There was no breach of the principle of proportionality in the Council's view that improvements in the health and safety of workers could not be achieved by less restrictive measures.

4. ENFORCEMENT OF E.C. LAW

Member States' obligations under Article 5

KEY PRINCIPLE: *Member States must take all appropriate measures to ensure fulfilment of the obligations arising from the Treaty or from secondary legislation. They must facilitate the E.C.'s tasks and abstain from measures which could jeopardise the objectives of the Treaty: Article 5.*

Commission v. Greece (Case 272/86) 1988

The Commission requested information from the Greek Government relating to cereal imports during enforcement proceedings under Article 169. Greece failed to supply information at both the informal and formal stages (see p. 30).

HELD: (ECJ) Failure to supply the information amounted to a failure to facilitate the achievement of the E.C.'s tasks under Article 5. [1988] E.C.R. 4875.

COMMENTARY
Article 5 lies at the heart of the Member States' obligations to implement and apply E.C. law. It is directly effective and is frequently cited by the ECJ. See *e.g. Von Colson* (Case 14/83) (see p. 8) and *Francovich* (Joined Cases C-6 & 9/90). As the E.C. lacks the mechanisms necessary to enforce E.C. law (with the exception of the new power to fine under Article 171: see p. 32 below) this obligation is transferred to the Member States under Article 5.

Actions under Article 169

KEY PRINCIPLE: *If the Commission considers that a Member State has failed to fulfil an obligation under the Treaty, it shall deliver a reasoned opinion on the matter after giving the state concerned the opportunity to submit its observations. If the state concerned does not comply with the opinion within the period laid down, the Commission may bring the matter before the ECJ: Article 169.*

KEY PRINCIPLE: *As the reasoned opinion sets out the scope of the judicial proceedings under Article 169, both sets of documents must be founded on the same grounds and submissions.*

Commission v. Italy (Case 31/69) 1970

(1) The Commission informed the Italian Government by a letter dated July 12, 1986 that it had failed to comply with various regulations over refunds under the Common Agricultural Policy (CAP). In the reasoned opinion delivered in

November 1968 the Commission found that Italy was in breach of the obligations under the Regulations. When proceedings were issued in the ECJ they included references to infringement of two regulations of June 1968 which had not been set out in the reasoned opinion.

HELD: (ECJ) Even if the Member State concerned does not consider it necessary to avail itself of the opportunity to submit its observations, such an opportunity constitutes an essential guarantee under the Treaty and amounts to an essential procedural requirement in proceedings under Article 169. The alleged failure deriving from the regulations of June 1968 must be excluded from the proceedings. [1970] E.C.R. 25.

COMMENTARY
(1) Article 169 provides a two-stage mechanism (the administrative and judicial stages) for the Commission to bring proceedings against a Member State which has infringed an obligation under E.C. law. During the administrative stage the Commission sends a letter setting out the breach and negotiates with the state in question. If the matter is unresolved the Commission may issue a reasoned opinion.
(2) The reasoned opinion must contain "a coherent statement of reasons which led the Commission to believe that the state in question has failed to fulfil an obligation under the Treaty": *Commission v. Italy* (*Pigmeat*) (Case 7/61). It must also specify the action required to remedy the breach and any period for implementation.
(3) Non–compliance with the opinion entitles the Commission to start formal proceedings in the ECJ (the judicial stage). The decision to proceed is a matter for the discretion of the Commission: *Star Fruit v. Commission* (Case 247/87). (4) While there has been a significant increase in the number of formal letters of notice of infringements (1209 letters in 1993 compared with 960 in 1990), more than half the cases are settled before the reasoned opinion is issued. About 70 cases a year reach the ECJ for decison under the formal procedure.

KEY PRINCIPLE: *Force majeure is no defence to an action under Article 169.*

Commission v. Italy (Case 101/84) 1986
Italy failed to submit statistical returns to the Commission from 1979 in relation to the carriage of goods contrary to Directive

78/546. The Italian Government put forward a defence of *force majeure*, claiming that it had been unable to comply following the destruction in a bomb blast of the vehicle register at the Data Processing Centre of the Ministry of Transport.

HELD: (ECJ) While the bomb attack may originally have amounted to *force majeure*, the ensuing difficulties had only lasted for a certain time. The administration had failed to exercise due diligence to replace the equipment and collect the data. The Italian Government could not, therefore, rely on the event to justify its continuing failure to comply. [1985] E.C.R. 1077.

COMMENTARY

Unless there has been a procedural flaw in the Commission's action, defences to actions in the ECJ under Article 169 have rarely succeeded. This is due to the strength of the Commission's case when proceedings reach the judicial stage, as complaints which are not well founded are normally resolved at the administrative stage.

KEY PRINCIPLE: *Practical difficulty in implementation is not a defence to enforcement proceedings.*

Commission v. U.K. (Case 128/78) 1979

Regulation 1463/70 provided for the installation of tachographs (to record rest periods and duration of driving) in vehicles used to carry passengers and goods on roads. It was due for implementation by January 1, 1976. The United Kingdom introduced a voluntary scheme to record the information and stated that it did not intend to implement the Regulation fully for economic, industrial and practical considerations.

HELD: (ECJ) Difficulties of implementation cannot be accepted as a justification. In permitting Member States to profit from membership of the E.C., the Treaty places on them the obligation to observe its rules. For a state to break the rules unilaterally is a breach of the principle of solidarity under Article 5. [1979] E.C.R. 419.

COMMENTARY

(1) Italy unsuccessfully argued that it should have a defence to proceedings arising out of non-implementation of a directive due to its frequent changes of government which prevented

the adoption of national legislation: *Commission v. Italy* (Case 28/81). Italy has been the most persistent offender in terms of Article 169 actions. It has sought to remedy the problem by passing a statute which annually transposes all E.C. directives (verbatim) into national law.

(2) If the ECJ finds that the state is in breach it will require the defaulting state to take the necessary steps to comply with the judgment: Article 171. After amendment of Article 171 by the TEU, if the state concerned does not comply, the Commission may issue a reasoned opinion after following a repetition of the procedure under Article 169 specifying the points of non-compliance. Non-compliance with the reasoned opinion entitles the Commission to bring the case before the ECJ which may impose a lump sum or penalty payment.

KEY PRINCIPLE: *The ECJ may prescribe the necessary interim measures in any cases before it: Article 184.*

Commission v. U.K. (Case 221/89R) 1989

For facts, see Chapter 1, p. 5.

HELD: (ECJ) The United Kingdom must suspend the offending provisions of the Merchant Shipping Act 1988, pending the determination of the proceedings under Article 169.

COMMENTARY
Applications for interim relief are normally heard before the President of the ECJ, who has the discretion to refer cases to the full court, if necessary.

Actions between Member States under Article 170

KEY PRINCIPLE: *Where a Member State considers that another Member State is in breach of E.C. law it may bring the matter before the ECJ if it has put the case before the Commission which has not acted within three months of the reasoned opinion: Article 170.*

France v. U.K. (Re Fishing Net Mesh Sizes) (Case 141/78)

France complained to the Commission about United Kingdom measures on fishing net mesh sizes. When the Commission did not proceed in the ECJ under Article 169 France brought the matter before the ECJ under Article 170.

HELD: (ECJ) The United Kingdom was in breach of E.C. law on fishing net mesh sizes. [1979] E.C.R. 2923.

COMMENTARY
Member States prefer to leave the resolution of their disputes with other states in the hands of the Commission, thus avoiding direct confrontation. Article 170 provides a mechanism for an aggrieved state to pursue its action directly against another state when the Commission has not acted on a reasoned opinion. Although proceedings have been commenced in a few other cases under Article 170, *France v. U.K.* is the only one resulting in an order against another state.

Specific enforcement proceedings

Actions under Article 93(2) on illegal state aids

KEY PRINCIPLE: *The Commission may issue a decision requiring a state to change or abolish illegal state aid within a specified time. Failure to comply entitles the Commission or any interested state to bring the matter before the ECJ: Article 93(2).*

British Aerospace and Rover Group Holdings plc v. Commission (Case C-292/90) 1992

The Commission had issued a decision requiring the United Kingdom Government to recover payments considered to be illegal state aid made to the Rover Group before its takeover by British Aerospace. While the aid to Rover to absorb debts had been approved by the Commission, provided no further aid was granted, additional unauthorised financial concessions ("sweeteners" of £44.4 million) were made by the United Kingdom Government to British Aerospace. British Aerospace and Rover sought annulment of part of the decision in the ECJ.

HELD: (ECJ) If the Commission considered that the United Kingdom had not complied with conditions in the decision and had paid further aid, it should have instituted proceedings directly against the United Kingdom under Article 93(2), and given notice to the parties concerned to submit their comments. The decision was annulled in relation to the requirement to recover the additional payment of £44.4 million. [1992] E.C.R. I-493.

COMMENTARY

After the judgment the Commission reopened proceedings on a proper basis under Article 93(2), treating the payment as aid. An out-of-court settlement was reached with the United Kingdom Government, as a result of which the sum was agreed to be repaid with interest.

Challenge under Article 225 to the use of expedited procedures

Key Principle: *Where it considers that a state is acting improperly, the Commission may challenge the action of a state which has brought expedited proceedings under Article 223 or 224: Article 225.*

Commission v. Greece (Case C-120/94R) 1994

The Commission sought interim relief in relation to the closure by Greece of its border with the former Yugoslavian Republic of Macedonia, pending the hearing of the main action (Case C-120/94).

HELD: (ECJ) Interim relief was refused. The ECJ considered that the interpretation of Articles 223–225 was uncertain and did not accept that there was an urgent prima facie case for relief. [1994] E.C.R. I-3037.

COMMENTARY

Member States may derogate from the Treaty under Articles 223 and 224: (a) to protect essential interests of their security connected with production and trade in arms, munitions and war materials, (b) where there is serious internal disturbance affecting the maintenance of law and order, and (c) in the event of a serious balance of payments crisis. Member States must co-operate closely with the Commission to avoid improper use of these powers.

5. JUDICIAL REVIEW OF THE ACTS OF THE E.C. INSTITUTIONS

Action for annulment under Article 173

Reviewable acts

KEY PRINCIPLE: *The ECJ may review the legality of acts adopted jointly by the E.P. and the Council, of acts of the Council, of the Commission and of the European Central Bank (ECB), and of acts of the E.P. intended to produce legal effects* vis-à-vis *third parties: Article 173, as amended by the TEU.*

Parti Ecologise ("Les Verts") v. E.P. (Case 294/83) 1986

Prior to amendment by the TEU Article 173 did not expressly provide that acts of the E.P. may be challenged. Les Verts (the Green Party) sought under Article 173 to challenge the allocation of funds by the Bureau of the E.P. to fight the 1984 European elections.

HELD: (ECJ) An action for annulment may lie against measures adopted by the E.P. where they are intended to produce legal effects *vis-à-vis* third parties. The allocation was annulled. [1986] E.C.R. 1339.

COMMENTARY
The decision in '*Les Verts*' has been incorporated verbatim in the amended version of Article 173(1), reflecting the increased involvement of the E.P. in the decision-making process. See the pre-T.E.U. decision in *Luxembourg v. E.P.* (Case 230/81), [1983] E.C.R. 255, in which the ECJ annulled a resolution of the E.P. to move its seat from Luxembourg to Brussels, based on an action under the ECSC Treaty which recognised the power to review acts of the E.P.

KEY PRINCIPLE: *The ECJ will look at the substance rather*

*than the form of a measure to determine whether it is intended
to have legal effect.*

Cimenteries v. Commission (Noordwijk's Cement Accord) (Cases 8–11/66) 1967

Various undertakings enjoyed exemption from fines under a
regulation in relation to competition. They were exposed to
penalties when the Commission changed its practice in a notice
sent out in a registered letter.

HELD: (ECJ) (1) The measure affected the undertakings'
interests by changing their legal position.
(2) It was not a mere opinion but a decision intended to
produce legal effects and must be considered a reviewable
act. [1967] E.C.R. 75.

COMMENTARY
(1) In *Cimenteries* and '*Les Verts*' the ECJ has recognised a
category of reviewable acts known as "acts *sui generis*", not
appearing in Article 189 (which refers specifically to regulations, directives and decisions).
(2) Other examples of reviewable acts include:

   (a) discussions of guidelines before the signing of the Eur-
       opean Road Transport Agreement: *Commission v.
       Council (Re Erta)* (Case 22/70);
   (b) a code of conduct issued by the Commission concern-
       ing the administration of the Structural Fund: *France v.
       Commission* (Case C-303/90).

(3) Applicants, both privileged and non-privileged, must bring
a claim for annulment within two months of publication of the
measure, or of notification to the applicant, or of the day on
which the applicant had knowledge of the measure (if not
notified): Article 173(3). Outside the time limit it may be easier
to bring a challenge under Article 184 (see p. 43).

KEY PRINCIPLE: *Certain "acts" may be so seriously
affected by defects of form or procedure that they are non-
existent and incapable of annulment.*

Commission v. BASF A.G. (Case C-137/92 P) 1992

The original text of a decision imposing fines on various chemical companies had been altered after its adoption. Also it had only been adopted in three of the official languages, leaving it to the Commissioner to adopt versions in the other languages. The CFI considered the decision to be so defective in form as to be non-existent. The Commission appealed to the ECJ.

HELD: (ECJ) The decision was defective but not sufficiently tainted by irregularity as to be non-existent. The original measure was annulled. A measure would be non-existent where it was "tainted by an irregularity whose gravity is so obvious that it cannot be tolerated by the Community legal order". [1994] E.C.R. I-2555.

COMMENTARY
(1) Acts of the E.C. institutions are presumed to be lawful. Only in exceptional circumstances will an act be found to be non—existent. (2) Other, less exceptional, examples of non-reviewable acts include: (a) a reasoned opinion under Article 169: *Commission v. Italy (Pigmeat)* (Case 7/61); (b) "comfort" letters issued by the Commission in competition cases, stating that an undertaking is not in breach of Article 85 (1) or is exempt: *Lancôme v. Etos B.V. (Perfumes)* (Case 99/79).

Locus standi: the right to challenge

KEY PRINCIPLE: *Member States, the Council and the Commission may bring actions for annulment before the ECJ on specified grounds. The E.P. and the ECB (after amendment by the TEU) may bring actions on the same grounds for the purpose of protecting their prerogatives: Article 173 (2) and (3).*

E.P. v. Council ("Chernobyl") (Case C-70/88) 1990

The E.P. challenged the legal basis of a Council regulation on the permitted level of radioactive contamination in foodstuffs following the Chernobyl explosion.

HELD: (ECJ) The ECJ shall have jurisdiction in actions brought by the E.P. or the ECB for the purpose of protecting their prerogatives. [1990] E.C.R. I–2041.

COMMENTARY

(1) Prior to amendment by the TEU, Article 173 did not explicitly recognise any entitlement by the E.P. to seek annulment. The '*Chernobyl*' decision partly overruled an earlier decision in *E.P. v. Council ("Comitology")* (Case 302/87) in which the ECJ had ruled that the E.P. could not challenge under Article 173 but only under Article 175. The amended version of Article 173 incorporates verbatim the wording in '*Chernobyl*'.

(2) The Member States and E.C. institutions are known as "privileged" applicants as they do not have to show that a measure is addressed to them or otherwise concerns them directly.

(3) It is more difficult for non-privileged applicants (natural or legal persons) to establish *locus standi*. An individual may only challenge:

(a) a decision addressed to himself (*e.g.* a competition decision by the Commission);

(b) a decision in the form of regulation (*i.e.* a measure equivalent to a decision);

(c) a regulation or decision addressed to another person which is of direct and individual concern to himself: Article 173(4).

KEY PRINCIPLE: *Only decisions or measures equivalent to decisions may be challenged.*

International Fruit N.V. (No. 1) v. Commission (Cases 41–44/70)

The applicant sought to challenge a regulation which prescribed the number of import licences for a particular period on the basis of previous applications.

HELD: (ECJ) As the regulation applied to a finite number of people identifiable from their previous applications it had the character of a decison and could be challenged. [1971] E.C.R. 411.

COMMENTARY

A regulation applies generally to categories of persons whereas a decision (or measure with the character of a decision) binds those to whom it is addressed, *i.e* named or identifiable individuals. Some regulations are hybrid in that they apply generally but operate as decisions for certain individuals.

KEY PRINCIPLE: *If the measure is not addressed to the applicant, it must be of direct and individual concern to him.*

Toepfer K.G. v. Commission (Cases 106 & 107/63) 1965

The applicant, an importer of maize, sought an import licence from the German Government. The German Government refused, seeking authorisation from the Commission for the safeguard measures it had taken. A Commission decision addressed to Germany approved the safeguard measures and the Government's refusal to grant all existing applicants a licence.

HELD: As the decision affected only existing applicants it was of individual concern to the applicant. The decision was annulled. [1965] E.C.R. 405.

Plaumann & Co. v. Commission (Case 25/62)

P, a major importer of clementines, sought to challenge a Commission decision addressed to the German Government refusing to allow the Government to reduce the duty on clementines imported from outside the E.C.

HELD: To establish individual concern the applicant must show that he is affected by the decision as a result of factors particularly relevant to him, not because he is a member of a class affected by the measure. The application was inadmissible. [1963] E.C.R. 95.

COMMENTARY
(1) The difference between the locus standi of the applicants in *Toepfer* and *Plaumann* is that T could be identified as a member of a closed class of persons affected by the decision whereas P could not. (Anyone could import clementines.)
(2) In a few cases the ECJ has demonstrated a liberal approach to *locus standi*. In *Piraiki-Patraiki* (Case 11/82) Greek producers of cotton were found to be individually concerned in a Commission decision, due mainly to the obligation in the

Greek Act of Accession to take such interests into account.
See also *Sofrimport v. Commission* (Case C-152/88): Importers with goods in transit could challenge a regulation which
had to take account of their interests.
(3) Contrast *Spijker Kwasten N.V. v. Commission* (Case 231/
82): Commission decision to allow a Dutch import ban on
Chinese brushes could not be challenged by a previous
import licence holder.

KEY PRINCIPLE: *The fact that a general legislative measure
applies to traders in a general way does not necessarily prevent individual traders from being individually concerned.*

Codorniu v. Council (Case C-309/89) 1993

C sought to challenge a Regulation reserving the word "crémant" for high-quality sparkling wines from specific regions in
France and Luxembourg. C was a major producer of similar
sparkling wines in Spain where it held a trade mark, and the
largest producer of wines labelled "crémant" in the E.U.

HELD: (ECJ) The applicant was individually concerned
because the reservation to producers in France and Luxembourg interfered with C's intellectual property rights. [1994]
E.C.R. I-1853.

COMMENTARY
(1) This decision departs from the previous case law of the
ECJ in that there was no suggestion that the Regulation had
been adopted with the applicant in mind.
(2) Jurisdiction to hear Article 173 applications brought by
non—privileged applicants passed to the CFI in August 1993.
So far the CFI has followed the pre-*Codorniu*, more restrictive
approach of the ECJ in refusing to accept that a claim to *locus
standi* could be based on a disadvantageous competitive
position. (See *Campo Edro Industrial v. Council* (Case T-
472/93) in which a regulation gave aid in sugar pricing to
producers of sugar from cane and beet but not to isoglucose
producers. Despite being the sole Spanish producers of isoglucose, the applicants were denied *locus standi* to challenge
the regulation.)

Grounds for challenge

KEY PRINCIPLE *A measure may be challenged under Article 173 if an essential procedural requirement is infringed.*

Roquette Frères S.A. v. Council (Case 138/79) 1980

The Council sent the E.P. a draft regulation fixing a quota for isoglucose producers for consultation in March 1979, asking for its views during April, so that the measure could be adopted by July. This would only have been possible if the E.P. had convened a special session but no such request was made by the Council or Commission. The measure was adopted by the Council in June 1979, with reference in the Preamble to the fact that the E.P. had been "consulted". R, a member of a closed group of isoglucose producers, sought to challenge the regulation.

HELD: (ECJ) Failure to consult the E.P., as required under Article 43(2) of the Treaty, was a breach of an essential procedural requirement. The regulation was annulled. [1980] E.C.R. 3393.

COMMENTARY
(1) Wrongly identifying the legal basis of a measure may lead to failure to consult the E.P. (See chapter 2).
(2) Failure to specify the legal basis of a measure may also be regarded as breach of an essential procedural requirement: *Commission v. Council* (Case 45/86), as may failure to state the reasons for a decision: *Germany v. Commission (Re Tariff Quotas on Wine)* (Case 24/62).
(3) A measure may also be challenged under Article 173 on grounds of lack of competence (similar to *ultra vires* in English law), infringement of the E.C. Treaty or any rule relating to its application, or misuse of power.

KEY PRINCIPLE: *A measure may be annulled where it is in breach of a general principle of E.C. law.*

Transocean Marine Paint Association v. E.C. Commission (Case 17/74) 1974

The Commission issued a measure in relation to the renewal of an exemption from the competition rules policy without providing an opportunity for the members of the Association to be heard. The Association argued that the measure should be annulled because it had been denied a hearing.

HELD: (ECJ) A person whose interests are affected by a decision by a public authority such as the Commission considering an exemption must be given an opportunity to submit his observations. The offending part of the measure was annulled. [1974] E.C.R. 1063.

COMMENTARY

This case provides an example of the ECJ's adoption of a general principle from the domestic law of the Member States: in this case, the United Kingdom (*audi alterem partem*). Infringement of a rule to the Treaty's application is interpreted liberally by the ECJ to cover any general principle of law, whether in international law, in the domestic legal systems of the Member States or in the general principles recognised by the ECJ (see Chapter 3).

Action for inactivity under Article 175

KEY PRINCIPLE: *If the E.P., Council or Commission fails to act on an infringement of the Treaty, the Member States and other institutions of the E.C. may bring an action before the ECJ to have the failure established: Article 175.*

E.P. v. Council (Case 13/83) 1985

The E.P. sought to challenge the failure of the Council to implement a common transport policy under Article 74 and to reach a decision on 16 Commission proposals on transport.

HELD: (ECJ) While there was no enforceable obligation to implement a common transport policy under Article 174, the Council was required to act to implement the freedoms expressed in Articles 75, 59, 50 and 61 within the transitional periods (end of 1961). To be enforceable obligations must be sufficiently defined to allow the ECJ to establish whether failure to adopt them is lawful.

COMMENTARY

This obligation mirrors that in Article 173. Rules on *locus standi* are similar, with the E.C. institutions in a privileged position, relative to individuals. Article 175 was amended by the TEU to include the E.P. and the ECB, as in Article 173.

KEY PRINCIPLE: *An individual may bring proceedings under Article 175 where an institution has failed to address to him or her an act other than a recommendation or opinion.*

Bethell v. Commission (Case 246/81) 1982

Lord Bethell sought to force the Commission to apply the competition rules against various European airlines. As this sector was outside Regulation 17 Lord Bethell had no entitlement to insist that the Commission carry out an investigation.

HELD: The applicant was not directly and individually concerned and could not challenge the Commission's inaction under Article 175, nor its refusal to act under Article 173. [1982] E.C.R. 2277.

COMMENTARY
No action may be brought under Article 175 unles the institution has first been called upon to act. It has two months in which to act or define its position, after which the applicant has a further two months in which to bring an action. A successful action under either Article 175 or 173 requires the institution to take the necessary steps to implement the judgment (Article 176). There are no sanctions for non-compliance.

Indirect challenge under Article 184

KEY PRINCIPLE: *Despite the expiry of the time limit under Article 173(5) (that is, two months from the date of adoption) any party may plead that a regulation is inapplicable on the grounds set out in Article 173(2).*

Italy v. Council and Commission (Case 32/65) 1966

Italy brought proceedings under Article 173 to annul a regulation and indirectly challenged two further regulations under Article 184. The Commission raised the issue of whether a Member State may make an indirect challenge.

HELD: (ECJ) As the regulations were not relevant to the issue

in question the challenge under Article 184 was dismissed.
[1966] E.C.R. 389.

COMMENTARY
(1) The ECJ did not rule on the entitlement of a Member State
to make an indirect challenge under Article 184.
(2) Article 184 applies only to regulations. However, it is substance not form which indicates the true character of a measure. (See *Simmenthal v. Commission* (Case 92/78) in which
the ECJ held that a general notice of invitation to tender was
normative in character and thus capable of indirect challenge
under Article 184.)
(3) The effect of a successful challenge under Article 184 will
lead to the regulation in question being declared inapplicable
and any subsequent measure void.

6. LIABILITY OF THE E.C. INSTITUTIONS

Non-contractual Liability

KEY PRINCIPLE: *The E.C. must, in accordance with the
general principles common to the laws of the Member States,
make good any damage caused by its institutions or by its
servants in performance of their duties (Article 215(2)).*

Lütticke v. Commission (Case 4/69) 1966
L sued the Commission for damages under Article 215(2),
claiming that it had failed to require the German Government
to change a disputed provision of national law. Under the
German measure in question L was obliged to pay taxes which
he alleged contravened E.C. law.

HELD: (ECJ) There was no wrongful act or omission. The
Commission had done all that it could in negotiating with the
German Government. Non-contractual (tortious) liability is
established under Article 215 where there is:

(a) a wrongful act or omission by an E.C. institution or its
servants;

(b) damage to the applicant;
(c) a causal connection between the wrongful act or omission and the damage. [1971] E.C.R. 325.

COMMENTARY
(1) *Lütticke* establishes that a claim for damages under Article 215(2) is an independent action. It departs from the previous approach of the ECJ in *Plaumann* (see Chapter 5) that annulment proceedings must be brought (under Article 173, 175 or 184) before a claim may be pursued under Article 215(2).
(2) Under Article 178 the ECJ has jurisdiction in compensation claims under Article 215(2). Jurisdiction was transferred to the CFI in September 1993.
(3) Unlike non-contractual liability, there is no specific set of rules governing breach of contract under E.C. law. Under Article 215(1) the contractual liability of the E.C. institutions is governed by the law applicable to the contract in question.

KEY PRINCIPLE: *Failure of administration* ("faute de service") *is a wrongful act or omission for which the E.C. is vicariously liable under Article 215(2).*

Richez-Parise v. Commission (Joined Cases 19/69, etc.) 1969

Some members of staff of the Commission were given wrong information about pensions, as a result of which they decided to take early retirement. Although the Commission discovered the mistake it did not seek to correct the information. The officials sued the Commission under Article 215(2).

HELD: (ECJ) Even though the giving of the advice originally was not wrongful, failure to correct the information was a *"faute de service"*. The Commission was liable to compensate members of staff who had relied on its advice. [1970] E.C.R. 325.

KEY PRINCIPLE: *A negligent act by a servant is a wrongful act for which the E.C. will be vicariously liable provided it is performed in the course of his duties* (faute de personne).

Sayag v. Leduc (Case 5/68) 1968

Sayag was an engineer employed by Euratom. While driving to visit an atomic plant in Belgium he injured someone in a road accident. The Belgian court made an Article 177 reference to the ECJ.

HELD: (ECJ) Driving a motor vehicle is not an act performed in the course of duty unless it is necessary in an emergency or other exceptional circumstances. Euratom was not vicariously liable. [1969] E.C.R. 329.

COMMENTARY

The distinction between *faute de service*, a fault in the operation of the system, and *faute personnelle*, a personal fault by an individual reflects French administrative law. Thus in E.C. law vicarious liability attaches to *faute de service* and to *faute personnelle* where the wrongful act is closely connected to the individual's duties (*i.e.* not a "frolic of one's own"). As in French law, the E.C. institutions may be vicariously liable for matters which would be considered maladministration in English law.

Liability for legislation: the "Schoppenstedt Formula"

KEY PRINCIPLE: *The E.C. is not liable in relation to a legislative measure involving choices of economic policy unless a sufficiently serious breach of a superior rule of law for the protection of the individual has occurred.*

Zuckerfabrik Schoppenstedt v. Council (Case 5/71) 1971

The applicant, a sugar trader, sought compensation under Article 215(2) for damage suffered as a result of a regulation, claiming that the measure infringed another regulation and Article 40(3) (the principle of non-discrimination under the CAP). The Council objected, claiming that the action would undermine the system of judicial review under Article 173.

HELD: (ECJ) The ruling of the ECJ in *Lütticke* (see above) was approved and the application was declared admissible. However, the breach was not found to be "sufficiently flagrant". As a result the application failed. [1971] E.C.R. 975.

COMMENTARY

(1) Most E.C. law involves choices of economic policy. It is the ECJ's responsibility to examine the acts of the institutions to

determine when those acts should give rise to compensation to individuals. It is not intended that individuals should be protected from variations in the market.

(2) Although known as the "Schoppenstedt Formula", the principle stated above represents a reformulation by the ECJ in *Bayerische HNL v. Council and Commission* (Joined Cases 83/76, etc.), approving the decision in *Schoppenstedt*. (See below.)

(3) The principles governing liability of the E.C. institutions have been applied to the liability of the Member States for breaches of E.C. law under *Francovich*. (See Chapter 1.)

KEY PRINCIPLE: *There must be a breach of a superior principle of law.*

CNTA v. Commission (Case 74/74)

This case concerns the system for monetary compensation amounts (MCAs) payable to exporters under the CAP to compensate for fluctuations in exchange rates. CNTA entered into various export contracts before the system was abolished in France by the Commission, claiming to have based the contractual prices on the MCAs. CNTA claimed damages for the losses arising from the ending of the scheme from the Commission.

HELD: (ECJ) The regulation infringed the principle of legal certainty, in particular the principle of legitimate expectations. In the absence of overriding public interest the Commission had violated a superior rule of law by not taking transitional measures to protect the trader. However, as no actual loss had been suffered, no damages were awarded. [1975] E.C.R. 533.

COMMENTARY

The wrongful act was the failure to give reasonable notice, not the adoption of the regulation (which was not declared invalid). Other general principles which have been invoked in damages claims include proportionality and equality. (See Chapter 3.)

KEY PRINCIPLE: *The breach must be sufficiently serious.*

Bayérische HNL v. Council and Commission (Cases 83/76, etc.) 1978

In order to use up the skimmed milk powder "mountain" the Council adopted a regulation requiring animal feed producers to buy skimmed milk powder from E.C. intervention agencies. This was more expensive than soya, which had previously been used as feed. Some farmers brought actions in the national courts, leading to Article 177 references to the ECJ. Others claimed damages in the ECJ.

HELD: (ECJ) (1) (Under Article 177) The regulation was invalid because it infringed the principles of non-discrimination and proportionality. (2) (Under Article 215) There was a breach of a superior breach of law which was intended to protect the individual. However, the breach was not sufficiently serious; in a legislative field involving wide discretion the E.C. is not liable unless there has been a manifest and grave breach. Thus damages were not available to the farmers. [1978] E.C.R. 1209.

COMMENTARY

Despite the invalidity ruling under Article 177 it did not follow that the breach was serious enough to satisfy the Schoppenstedt Formula under Article 215.

KEY PRINCIPLE: *The rule of law must be intended for the protection of the individual.*

Kampffmeyer v. Commission (Joined Cases 5/66, etc.) 1967

The applicants, German grain importers, applied to the German authorities for a licence to import grain from France. The German authorities refused, suspending imports. The Commission confirmed the decision. Under Regulation 19 such applications could only be refused if a serious disturbance of the market was threatened. The applicants challenged the Commission decision under Article 173 in the ECJ and also sued the German Government in the national courts.

HELD: (ECJ) Although the rules of law in question were not of direct and individual concern to the applicant (under Article 173), the protection of individual interests such as the applicant's was intended. The application was admissible. As there was no serious threat to the market, the Commission decision was unjustified (*faute de service*) and was annulled. [1967] E.C.R. 245.

COMMENTARY
(1) A rule intended to benefit a class of persons may be found to benefit an individual.
(2) The ECJ deferred a decision on damages until the concurrent proceedings before the German courts were completed.
(3) The E.C. may not be liable where there is an overriding public interest. In *Mulder v. Commission* (Joined Cases C-104/89 and 37/90) milk producers who had no quota due to lack of production in the year preceding their application were given a quota based on 60 per cent of production in the year before that. *Held:* (ECJ) although the quota decision was illegal because it infringed the principle of legitimate expectations, the Council had taken account of a higher public interest in fixing the rate, without gravely and manifestly disregarding the limits of its discretionary power. [1992] E.C.R I-3061.

Damages

KEY PRINCIPLE: *Damages for loss of profits may be available against the E.C. institutions.*

CNTA v. Commission (Case 74/74) 1975
See p. 47.

HELD: (ECJ) A firm is entitled to compensation for losses caused by currency speculation where this has been caused by the E.C. [1975] E.C.R. 533.

COMMENTARY
The applicant was not in fact exposed to risk because its purchaser could pay in either French francs or American dollars. As the purchaser had paid in francs (with no exchange rate consequences) there was no actual loss. Traders cannot rely on the E.C. for protection against the operation of the market.

KEY PRINCIPLE: *An award of damages may be reduced by the contributory negligence of the applicant.*

Adams v. Commission (Case 145/83) 1985

Stanley Adams was employed in Switzerland by the pharmaceutical company, Hoffman-La Roche. He handed over documents to the Commission, as a result of which the company was found to have infringed Article 86 and fined. Adams had requested confidentiality from the Commission which failed to ensure that he was not identified from the documents. On returning to Switzerland from Italy where he had set up a business, Adams was arrested and charged with industrial espionage under Swiss law. Adams' wife committed suicide while her husband was in custody awaiting trial. Adams was convicted of industrial espionage and given a one year's suspended sentence. He claimed that his credit-worthiness had been destroyed, leading to the failure of his business in Italy.

HELD: (ECJ) The Commission was liable for breach of the principle of confidentiality and for failing to warn Adams of the risk of prosecution in Switzerland. The damages were reduced by one half due to Adams' carelessness in failing to inform the Commission of his whereabouts and in returning to Switzerland despite the risk of prosecution. [1985] E.C.R. 3539.

COMMENTARY

As there have been relatively few awards of damages made by the ECJ or CFI it is difficult to identify a set of principles from individual decisions, beyond stating that damages should not be too remote (*Lütticke*) and must be a sufficiently direct result of unlawful act or omission of an E.C. institution (*Dumortier Fils S.A. v. Council* (Joined Cases 64/76 etc.). Note the liberal limitation period (five years) for bringing a claim under Article 215(2) (Article 43 of the Statute of the Court), unlike the two month period for an annulment action under Article 173.

Concurrent Liability

KEY PRINCIPLE: *Where the national authority is primarily at fault the action should be brought in the national courts.*

Kampffmeyer v. Commission (Cases 5/66 etc.) 1967
See p. 48.

HELD: (ECJ) The amount of damages awarded against the Commission could not be finalised until K had completed proceedings before the German courts.

COMMENTARY
(1) The requirement to pursue a remedy in the national courts has been upheld in *Haegeman v. Commission* (Case 96/71). There are problems arising from this approach as the scope or availability of a remedy may vary between Member States.
(2) The ECJ has not been consistent on the need to exhaust national remedies before proceeding in the ECJ (now in the CFI). In *Krohn v. Commission* (Case 175/84) it was held to be appropriate to bring an action in the ECJ rather than the national courts where the national authorities, on Commission instructions, had refused an import licence.

7. PRELIMINARY RULINGS

Preliminary rulings under Article 177

KEY PRINCIPLE: *Article 177 is essential for the Community character of the law established by the Treaty and has the object of ensuring that in all circumstances, E.C. law is given the same interpretation in all states of the Community.*

Rheinmuhlen-Dusseldorf v. Einfuhr-und Vorratsstelle Getreide (Joined Cases 146 & 166/73) 1974
R, a German cereal exporter, unsuccessfully sought to rely on E.C. law in the Hessian Tax Court to obtain an export rebate. He appealed to the Federal Tax Court (Bundesfinanzhof) which quashed the decision of the lower court, holding that R was entitled to a rebate. The case was sent back to the Hessian Tax Court to decide certain points of fact. The Hessian Tax Court, although bound under German law by the decisions of the

Federal Tax Court, refused to follow the decision of the higher
court and referred several questions to the ECJ under Article
177. R appealed to the Federal Tax Court against the lower
court's decision to make a reference. The Federal Tax Court
then referred further questions to the ECJ to determine the
extent of a lower court's powers to make a reference in such
circumstances.

HELD: (ECJ) The power of a lower court to make a reference
cannot be abrogated by national law; the lower court must be
free to refer if it considers that the higher court's ruling could
lead to it giving a judgment contrary to E.C. law. [1974]
E.C.R. 33.

COMMENTARY
(1) Article 177 provides a mechanism which enables the ECJ
to give preliminary rulings on:

   (a) the interpretation of the E.C. Treaty;
   (b) the validity and interpretation of acts of the institu-
       tions of the E.C. Treaty and of the European Central
       Bank; and
   (c) the interpretation of the statutes of bodies established
       by an act of the Council.

(2) The procedure has been of great importance in the
development of E.C. Law. As the E.C. Treaty is a framework
(or "traité cadre") with little detail or definition, the ECJ has
used the procedure to explain and clarify its provisions. The
task of interpreting E.C. law has been described by Bingham
J. in the High Court as involving the "creative process of
supplying flesh to a spare and loosely constructed skeleton":
Customs and Excise v. Samex, 1983.
(3) The interpretations apply equally to all Member States,
irrespective of the origin of any individual reference, thus
ensuring uniformity of interpretation throughout the E.C. Article 177 rulings are interlocutory rulings provided by the ECJ
(but not the CFI). After the question has been formulated by
the national court, proceedings should be suspended pending
the ruling. (This may take up to two years.) The national court
should then apply the ruling to the issues in question.

Discretionary References

Court or Tribunal

KEY PRINCIPLE: *Any court or tribunal of a Member State has the power to make a reference under Article 177 to the ECJ.*

Broekmeulen v. Huisarts Registratie Commissie (Case 246/80) 1981

A Dutch Appeals Committee for General Medicine (not regarded as a court or tribunal under Dutch law) refused B's application to practise as a doctor in the Netherlands. During the course of a reference the ECJ considered whether the Committee was a court or tribunal for the purpose of Article 177.

HELD: (ECJ) Where there is no right of appeal to the ordinary courts, the Appeals Committee, which operates with the consent of the public authorities and with their co-operation and which delivers decisions which are final after an adversarial procedure, must be regarded as a court or tribunal for the purpose of Article 177. [1981] E.C.R. 2311.

COMMENTARY

For a body to be considered a court or tribunal under Article 177 it is essential that the body in question exercises a judicial function (by making legally binding decisions), is competent to make a reference and is subject to control by public authorities. These elements were found by the ECJ to be lacking in *Nordsee Deutsch Hochseefischerei GmbH* (Case 102/81) where an arbitrator was appointed without participation of public authorities, under a contract in which recourse to arbitration was voluntary.

Necessity

KEY PRINCIPLE: *Where a question of interpretation or validity of E.C. law is raised before a court or tribunal of a Member State, that court or tribunal may, if it considers that a question is necessary to enable it to give judgment, request the ECJ to give a ruling on it (Article 177(2)).*

CILFIT Srl. and Lanificio di Gavardo Spa. v. Ministry of Health (Case 283/81) 1982

Wool importers disputed a health inspection levy imposed by the Italian Government on wool imported from outside the E.C., arguing that wool is an animal product (for which charges could not be imposed by regulation) and therefore not subject to such a charge. The Italian Government claimed that the interpretation of "animal product" was obvious under the *acte clair* principle, in which case no reference under Article 177 was necessary. The Italian Supreme Court referred the question to the ECJ.

HELD: (ECJ) A reference to the ECJ is *not* necessary where:
(1) the question of E.C. law is irrelevant;
(2) the question has already been decided by the ECJ; and
(3) the correct interpretation is so obvious as to leave no scope for doubt. [1982] E.C.R. 3415.

COMMENTARY

(1) While the ruling in CILFIT was formulated in response to a question concerning mandatory references under Article 177(3) (see below), it applies also to discretionary references. The '*acte clair*' doctrine derives from French administrative law: international treaties need not be referred to the government for interpretation if the meaning is clear.
(2) In *Bulmer v. Bollinger* (C.A., 1974) [1974] 2 All E.R. 1226, Lord Denning drew up guidelines for the United Kingdom courts in making Article 177 references. The guidelines, though not binding, were treated as influential. Factors to be taken into account were stated to include the existence of a previous ECJ ruling, the conclusiveness of the reference to the judgment, the need to establish the facts, delay, the wishes of the parties and costs. Lord Denning's guidelines have been criticised as unduly restrictive. They should not be followed where they conflict with *CILFIT*.
(3) The Court of Appeal has recently ruled that three factors must be present if a reference is to be made: the facts must be clear, the provision of E.C. law must be conclusive to the determination of the case and the judge must consider whether he himself can resolve the question of E.C. law with complete confidence (*R. v. International Stock Exchange of the U.K. and the Republic of Ireland, ex p. Else* [1931] 1 All E.R. 420.

Mandatory References

KEY PRINCIPLE: *Where a question of interpretation or validity of E.C. Law is raised before any court or tribunal of a Member State against whose decisions there is no judicial remedy, that court or tribunal shall bring the matter before the ECJ (Article 177(3)).*

Costa v. ENEL (Case 6/64) 1964

Several questions were referred to the ECJ by the Italian small claims court (see Chapter 1 p. 4). As the sum claimed was very low there was no right of appeal to a higher national court.

HELD: (ECJ) National courts against whose decisions, as in the present case, there is no judicial remedy must refer the matter to the ECJ. [1964] E.C.R. 585.

COMMENTARY

Identification of the courts which are covered by the obligation to refer under Article 177(3) has been controversial. United Kingdom courts have been reluctant to accept that courts other than the House of Lords are obliged to refer. The position of the Court of Appeal and other lower courts has been difficult to determine. It may be impossible to know until a case is concluded whether the Court of Appeal is the court of last resort or not (*i.e.* whether leave to appeal against a decision of the C.A. will be granted by the C.A. itself or by the H.L.). The ECJ has not ruled on this point. The present uncertainties are illustrated by *S.A. Magnavision N.V. v. General Optical Council.* The High Court had refused leave to appeal to the House of Lords against conviction on a point of E.C. law (*Magnavision No. 1*, QBD, 1987). The Divisional Court in *Magnavision No. 2* (QBD, 1987) refused leave to appeal on a point of public importance (whether the Divisional Court became a court of final resort when leave to appeal to the H.L. was refused), ruling that the matter was closed. The applicant was left without a remedy. While no clear precedent exists in English law the United Kingdom courts appear to be moving towards acceptance of the wide view as expressed in *Costa v. ENEL* rather than the narrow view in *Magnavision.*

KEY PRINCIPLE: *References under Article 177 are not precluded by the existence of a prior ruling of the ECJ on a similar point.*

Da Costa en Schake N.V. v. Nederlandse Belastagingenadministratie (Joined Cases 28–30/62) 1963

A Dutch court of last resort referred questions identical to those in *Van Gend en Loos* (see Chapter 1, p. 3) on which judgment had recently been given by the ECJ. The Commission argued that the reference should be dismissed for lack of cause, as no questions remained for interpretation.

HELD: (ECJ) Where an authoritative ruling has been made on an identical point, a national court need not refer. However, no national court may be deprived of the opportunity to refer a provision which has already been interpreted. [1963] E.C.R. 31.

COMMENTARY
The ECJ does not operate a formal doctrine of binding precedent. Nevertheless, it does tend in most cases to follow its own previous decisions. In *Da Costa* the Court stated that making a reference on a point materially identical to a previous ruling may "deprive the obligation [to refer under Article 177(3)] of its purpose and thus empty it of its substance". The national court was directed to the judgment in *Van Gend en Loos*. Where the ECJ intends to depart from its own previous decision it normally makes the change of direction very clear. (See, *e.g. Keck and Mithouard* (Joined Cases C-267 & 268/91) (Chapter 9, p. 66.)

Misuse of the Article 177 Procedure

KEY PRINCIPLE: *Questions referred by national courts must involve genuine issues of E.C. law or they will not be considered by the ECJ.*

Foglia v. Novella (No.1) (Case 104/79) (1980)

F and N, wine dealers in France and Italy, inserted a clause in their contract of sale not to pay any tax which contravened E.C. law. F sought to recover from N the tax incurred by a carrier of the goods in France. It appeared that the parties may

have artificially concocted the contractual terms and the litiga-
tion in order to obtain a ruling on the validity of the French
law.

HELD: (ECJ) It is the duty of the ECJ to supply rulings in
genuine disputes. To rule in circumstances such as the present
case would jeopardise the system by which individuals can
protect themselves against tax provisions contrary to the Treaty.
[1980] E.C.R. 745.

COMMENTARY

(1)The ECJ refused to rule in *Foglia v. Novella (No.1)* and
remitted the case to the national court. Undeterred, the Italian
court made a further attempt to refer the same questions to
the ECJ in *Foglia v. Novella (No.2)* (Case 244/80). Again the
ECJ refused to answer, stating that the Court must be espe-
cially vigilant when asked to consider the validity of the
national laws of another Member State. The decision has
been criticised as unhelpful to the national court faced with
a real, not a hypothetical problem (the validity of the tax under
E.C. law).

(2) The ECJ has declined to rule in a number of cases. See,
e.g. SPUC v. Grogan (Case C-159/90) in which no ruling was
made in relation to public policy and the availability of information about abortion services, because the information was
available without charge and so was outside the scope of
Article 59.

(3) Compare with *Dzodzi v. Belgium* (Joined Cases C-297/88
& 197/89) (application of E.C. social security rules outside the
E.C. where national law made reference to E.C. rules). The
ECJ was prepared to make a ruling in order to ensure the
uniform application of E.C. law.

Rulings on Validity

KEY PRINCIPLE: *While national courts may declare that a
provision of E.C. law is valid, only the ECJ may declare a
provision of E.C. law invalid.*

Foto-Frost v. Hauptzollamt Lubeck-Ost (Case 314/85) 1987

A German court referred to the ECJ the question of whether a
national court could declare invalid a provision of E.C. law (in

this case, a decision which appeared to conflict with a regulation).

HELD: (ECJ) National courts have no jurisdiction to declare that acts of E.C. institutions are invalid. [1987] E.C.R. 4199.

COMMENTARY
In *Foto-Frost* the ECJ stated that an exception to the rule might arise in the event of an applicant seeking an interim injunction (although no question had been referred on this point). The issue was taken up in *Zuckerfabrik* (see below).

KEY PRINCIPLE: *The national courts are not precluded by Article 189 of the Treaty from suspending enforcement of a national administrative measure adopted on the basis of an E.C. regulation.*

Zuckerfabrik Suderdithmarschen A.G. v. Hauptzollamt Itzehoe (Case C-143/88) 1991

Z, a sugar producer, complained that a German decision imposing a levy based on an E.C. regulation was invalid. The German court referred a number of questions to the ECJ, including the possible basis for the suspension of a national measure based on a regulation which may be invalid.

HELD: (ECJ) A national court may suspend a national measure adopted to implement an E.C. regulation if:

(1) the national court entertains serious doubts as to the validity of the E.C. measure and itself refers the question of validity to the ECJ (if this has not already been done);
(2) there is urgency and a threat of serious and irreparable damage to the applicant;
(3) the national court takes due account of the E.C.'s interests. [1991] E.C.R. I-415.

COMMENTARY
Due to the length of time required to obtain an Article 177 reference from the ECJ (up to two years) the need for an interim remedy pending final resolution of the issues has become great in a number of cases. In *R. v. Secretary of State for Transport, ex p. Factortame* the House of Lords applied the ruling of the ECJ in Case 213/89 (see Chapter

1) and suspended the offending parts of the Merchant Shipping Act 1988. The House of Lords held that interim relief was necessary to protect the rights of individuals under E.C. law.

8. FREE MOVEMENT OF GOODS

The Customs Union

KEY PRINCIPLE: *Member States are required under Article 9 of the Treaty to form a customs union. They must not introduce any new customs duties between Member States, nor must they increase existing duties (Article 12).*

Van Gend en Loos v. Nederlandse Administratie der Belastingen (Case 26/62) 1963

For facts see Chapter 1, p. 3.

HELD: (ECJ) Article 12 is directly effective. [1963] E.C.R. 1.

COMMENTARY

The customs union involves the prohibition between Member States of customs duties on imports and exports and of charges having equivalent effect, and the adoption of a customs tariff in relation to third countries (non-Member States) (Articles 12–17). *Van Gend en Loos* illustrates the importance attached by the ECJ to the customs union by recognising that individuals may enforce their rights under Article 12 before the national courts.

KEY PRINCIPLE: *A charge having equivalent effect which is disguised as a tax or levy is illegal under Article 12.*

Social Fonds voor de Diamantarbeiders v. S.A. C. Brachfeld (Cases 2 & 3/69) 1969

The Belgian Government imposed a levy on imported diamonds in order to provide social security benefits for diamond workers. An Article 177 reference was made to the ECJ.

HELD: (ECJ) The imposition of a charge on goods crossing a frontier is an obstacle to the free movement of goods. Such a levy is prohibited under Article 12 independently of its destination or purpose. [1969] E.C.R. 211.

COMMENTARY

If the diamond workers' welfare scheme had been funded through a non-discriminatory system of taxation without reference to imports it would have been permissible under Article 95 (see below).

Discriminatory Taxation

KEY PRINCIPLE: *No Member State may impose a tax directly or indirectly on products from another Member State greater than that applied to similar domestic products. Indirect protection through taxation of domestic products is also illegal: Article 95.*

Commission v. U.K. (Re Excise Duties on Wine) (No.1) (Case 170/78) 1980

The Commission sought a declaration under Article 169 that the United Kingdom had infringed Article 95 by imposing a higher excise duty on light wines than on beers.

HELD: (ECJ) Allowing for changing drinking habits and the increasing popularity of wine in the United Kingdom it is possible to regard wine and beer as similar products in competition with each other and to compare the taxation of each. No ruling was made pending further investigation. [1980] E.C.R. 417.

HELD (No.2) (Case 178/78A) 1983: (ECJ) (Following the investigation by the Commission) The United Kingdom tax system discriminated against imported wine so as to afford a protection to domestically produced beer, contrary to Article 95. [1983] E.C.R. 2265.

COMMENTARY

Article 95 allows Member States freedom to create their own internal systems of taxation provided there is no discrimination between Member States. Similar products may be taxed differently only where the distinction is objectively justified. In *Commission v. France* (Case 196/85) there was no breach when traditional sweet wines were taxed at a lower rate than ordinary wines to provide economic assistance to rural areas dependent on wine production.

(2) In *Humblot v. Directeur des Services Fiscaux* (Case 112/84) road tax was payable to the French Government at a higher rate on cars of more than 16 c-v, the highest engine capacity for cars made in France. A French taxpayer sought to recover the additional tax paid on a 36 c-v car imported from Germany. The ECJ held the system to be a breach of Article 95. An amended tax system was later found still to breach Article 95.

Quantitative Restrictions and Measures having Equivalent Effect

KEY PRINCIPLE: *Quantitative restrictions and all measures having equivalent effect are prohibited under Article 30.*

R. v. Henn and Darby (Case 34/79) 1980

The United Kingdom seized pornographic goods imported from the Netherlands. The importers were prosecuted and an Article 177 reference was made by the House of Lords.

HELD: (ECJ) A total ban is a quantitative restriction under Article 30. (The measure was in fact found to be justified under Article 36: see p. 68.) [1979] E.C.R. 3795.

COMMENTARY

Anything which restricts importation by reference to quantity (*e.g.* a quota system) is a quantitative restriction.

KEY PRINCIPLE: *All trading rules enacted by Member States which are capable of hindering, directly or indirectly, actually or potentially, intra-E.C. trade are to be considered as measures having an effect equivalent to quantitative restrictions.*

Procureur du Roi v. Dassonville (Case 8/74) 1974

Dassonville, a trader, imported Scotch whisky into Belgium from France without a certificate of origin, contrary to Belgian law. He was charged with a criminal offence but pleaded that the Belgian requirement contravened Article 30. An Article 177 reference was made.

HELD: (ECJ) In the absence of harmonisation, a Member State may take measures to prevent unfair practices provided they are reasonable and do not hinder inter-member trade. It was more difficult for a trader importing goods in circulation in another Member State to obtain a certificate than for an importer to do so when importing the goods directly from the state of production. Thus the requirement to obtain a certificate was a measure having equivalent effect and was illegal under Article 30. [1974] E.C.R. 837.

COMMENTARY

(1) *Dassonville* is important in that it defines what is meant by a "measure having equivalent effect" (MEQR). Further examples of MEQRs include inspection fees at frontiers and charges for storage pending inspections. Following the decision in *Keck and Mithouard* (see p. 66) a more restrictive approach has been taken by the ECJ to measures regarded as MEQRs.

(2) Directive 70/50 divides measures into distinctly effective measures (which do not apply equally to domestic and imported goods) and indistinctly effective measures (which apply alike to both domestic and imported goods).

(3) Under Article 3 of Directive 70/50 indistinctly applicable measures only infringe Article 30 when they are disproportionate (*i.e.* more restrictive than necessary to achieve their objective).

KEY PRINCIPLE: *Member States may not promote national products where this involves discrimination against imports.*

Commission v. Ireland (Case 249/81) 1982

A scheme was operated ("Buy Irish") to promote the sales of Irish goods to shoppers in Ireland. A symbol indicating Irish origin was attached to goods and an information service was available. According to the Irish Government the scheme was not particularly successful as the sale of imported products actually rose during the promotion period. The Commission brought an action against the Irish Government under Article 169.

HELD: (ECJ) If a measure is capable of restricting imports it is illegal under Article 30. [1982] E.C.R. 4005.

COMMENTARY

Contrast the "Buy Irish" case with *Apple and Pear Council v. Lewis* (Case 222/82) in which a Council funded by a levy on apple and pear growers in England and Wales was created to promote the consumption of English and Welsh varieties. Some growers refused to pay, claiming that the scheme infringed Article 30. The ECJ (under Article 177) held that it was permissible to promote a product by reference to its qualities, even where those qualities are typical of national production.

KEY PRINCIPLE: *There is no valid reason why goods which have been lawfully produced and marketed in one Member State should not be introduced into any other Member State (the principle of mutual recognition).*

Rewe-Zentral A.G. v. Bundesmonopolverwaltung fur Branntwein ("Cassis de Dijon") (Case 120/78 1979)

Cassis de Dijon is a blackcurrent liqueur originating in France where it contains 15 to 20 per cent alcohol by volume. German law required fruit liqueurs to have a minimum alcohol content of 25 per cent. While the measure was not discriminatory it clearly excluded French cassis from the German market. German importers challenged the measure in the national court which made an Article 177 reference.

HELD: In the absence of E.C. rules, the Member States may regulate the production and marketing of alcoholic drinks. Obstacles to movement within the E.C. arising from disparities between national laws relating to the marketing of the products must be accepted in so far as they may be necessary to satisfy mandatory requirements relating in particular to the effectiveness of fiscal supervision, the protection of public health, fairness of commercial transactions and the defence of the consumer. [1979] E.C.R. 649.

COMMENTARY

(1) The ECJ rejected German Government claims that a requirement for a higher alcohol content discouraged alcoholism and

that it protected consumers against unfair commercial practices. The requirement infringed the principle of proportionality and, while mandatory, was not necessary. Consumers
could be protected by being given information about the
alcoholic content on the label.

(2) The mandatory requirements in *Cassis* have provided a
basis for departing from Article 30 in cases involving *indistinctly* applicable measures. They were not satisfied in *Commission v. Germany* (Case 178/84) in which a long-standing
ban on additives in beer was found to be unjustifiable on
health grounds. Other unjustifiable measures have included
a restriction on the shape of bottles containing traditional
alcoholic drinks and a requirement to sell margarine in cubes.

(3) Note that *distinctly* applicable measures may only be justified under Article 36 (see p. 68).

(4) The principle of mutual recognition represents a widening
of the *Cassis* principle to cover all goods, not merely alcoholic
beverages. It has provided the basis for the single market
(1992) programme of directives to harmonise standards.

KEY PRINCIPLE: *National strategies to protect the environment may infringe Article 30.*

Commission v. Denmark (Case 302/86) 1988

Danish law required that beer and soft drinks could be sold
only in reusable containers, as part of a deposit-and-return
scheme on grounds of environmental protection. The scheme
was later modified to allow producers to market a limited
quantity of drinks in non-approved containers. The Commission brought an action under Article 169 in the ECJ, claiming
that the measure infringed Article 30.

HELD: (ECJ) Although protection of the environment is an
important objective, the quantitative restriction on beverages
which could be sold in non-approved containers had a disproportionate effect on importers from other E.C. states. Denmark
was in breach of Article 30. [1988] E.C.R. 4607.

COMMENTARY
This case illustrates the difficult position of a Member State
introducing a measure which can affect imports, in the
absence of common E.C. rules. Contrast the decision with

Oebel (Case 155/80) in which a Belgian law forbidding night working in bakeries was held not to infringe Article 30 because it did not affect imports.

KEY PRINCIPLE: *The regulation of Sunday trading falls within the discretion of Member States to make political and economic choices to accord with national or regional socio-cultural characteristics.*

Torfaen Borough Council v. B & Q plc (Case 145/88) 1989

The defendant was charged with trading on a Sunday contrary to the Shops Act 1950. The magistrates court referred to the ECJ the question of whether such a measure breached Article 30.

HELD: (ECJ) It is a legitimate part of socio-economic policy for Member States to regulate opening hours. Such rules do not infringe Article 30 provided they are not disproportionate and do not affect inter-member trade. [1989] E.C.R. 3851.

COMMENTARY
(1) *Torfaen* left many shops and local authorities in confusion over Sunday trading. Later decisions clarified the position. The ECJ stated unequivocally in *Stoke on Trent and Norwich City Council v. B & Q* (Cases C-169/91) that the prohibition in Article 30 does not apply to national legislation prohibiting retailers from opening their premises on Sundays. The Sunday trading laws did not discriminate against imports. Their legitimacy turned on proportionality (weighing national interests in achieving the objective against E.C. interests in the free movement of goods.
(2) A ban on the employment of labour in France and Belgium on Sundays was also outside Article 30: *Marchandise* (Case C-332/89) and *Conforama* (Case C-312/89).
(3) The Sunday Trading Act 1994 now permits shops in England and Wales below a certain floor area to trade freely on Sundays. Larger shops may trade for six hours between 10 a.m. and 6 p.m.

KEY PRINCIPLE: *Article 30 does not apply to selling arrangements by Member States which do not affect inter-member trade.*

Keck and Mithouard (Joined Cases C-267 & 268/91) 1993

K and M had resold goods at a loss contrary to French law. They claimed that the prohibition restricted the volume of sales of imported goods and so infringed Article 30. An Article 177 reference was made.

HELD: (ECJ) Contrary to what had previously been decided, the application to products from other Member States of national provisions restricting or partitioning certain selling arrangements does not hinder directly or indirectly, actually or potentially, trade between Member States within the meaning of the *Dassonville* judgment. [1993] E.C.R. I-6097.

COMMENTARY

(1) *Keck and Mithouard* signals a departure from the previous line of case law developed by the ECJ since *Cassis*. Traders had relied too heavily on Article 30 to challenge national measures restricting commercial freedom where there was no effect on imports. Member States should be free to adopt measures which do not affect inter-member trade.

(2) Later cases have confirmed this approach. In *Tankstation't Heukste Vof and Boermans* (Case C-401/92) Dutch rules on opening hours of shops in petrol stations were held to be outside Article 30. A similar finding was made in *Hunermund v. Landesapothekerkammer Baden-Wurttemberg* (Case C-292/92) (prohibition on promotion of para-pharmaceutical products outside pharmacies). See also *Belgapom v. ITM Belgium* and *Vocarex S.A.* (Case C-63/94). (Potatoes were sold at a loss contrary to Belgian law. *Held*: (ECJ) Article 30 does not apply to national legislation prohibiting sales at a very low profit margin.)

KEY PRINCIPLE: *Each case should be assessed on its merits to determine the actual or potential effect of national legislation in relation to Article 30.*

Neeltje v. Houtwipper (Case C-293/93) 1994

Dutch law required all precious metals to be hallmarked according to certain specifications before being offered for sale. Thus imported goods would require re-hallmarking on entering the Netherlands. An Article 177 reference was made.

HELD: (ECJ) While the hallmarking requirement was a mandatory measure to protect consumers and promote fair trading, it infringed Article 30 by requiring the fixing of a fresh hallmark where an equivalent hallmark had already been affixed in another Member State. [1994] E.C.R. I-4249.

COMMENTARY

Unlike *Keck and Mithouard* the measure in *Neeltje* discriminated against imports.

Quantitative Restrictions on Exports and Measures having Equivalent Effect

KEY PRINCIPLE: *Restrictions on exports will only breach Article 34 if they have as their object or effect the restriction of patterns of exports, providing an advantage to the home product or market.*

Groenveld v. Produktschap voor Vee en Vlees (Case 15/79) 1979

Dutch law prohibited all meat processors from stocking or processing horsemeat, in order to prevent the export of horsemeat to countries prohibiting its sale. Groenveld decided to make horsemeat sausages, contrary to Dutch law, claiming that the law infringed Article 34 by prohibiting the processing and exporting of horsemeat.

HELD: (ECJ) Article 34 did not apply to a rule which did not discriminate between goods for the home market and for export. [1989] E.C.R. 3967

COMMENTARY

(1) The *Cassis* justifications for restrictions on imports do not apply to exports. Whereas importers face a "dual burden", namely the requirements of the home state and of the importing state, exporters need only satisfy the requirements of the home state. Thus export restrictions may only be justified under Article 36.

(2) "Quantitative restrictions" and "measures having equivalent effect" have the same meanings for Article 34 as for Article 30.

Derogations from Articles 30 to 34

KEY PRINCIPLE: *Articles 30 to 34 do not preclude prohibitions on imports, exports or goods in transit justified on grounds of public morality, public policy or public security; the protection of life or health of humans, animals or plants; the protection of national treasures possessing artistic, historic or archaeological value; or the protection of industrial or commercial property. Such prohibitions must not constitute a means of arbitrary discrimination or a disguised restriction on trade between Member States: Article 36.*

KEY PRINCIPLE: *Restrictions on imports or exports may be justified on grounds of public morality.*

R. v. Henn and Darby (Case 34/79) 1979

See p. 61. The United Kingdom seized films and publications being imported from the Netherlands into the United Kingdom. The importers were prosecuted under customs and excise legislation with importing indecent and obscene articles. In their defence the importers claimed that the prohibition contravened Article 30 in that a stricter standard was being applied to imported than to domestic goods. An Article 177 reference was made.

HELD: (ECJ) A Member State may lawfully prohibit on grounds of public morality the importation from another Member State of indecent or obscene materials as understood by its domestic laws. A prohibition on imports which is stricter than the domestic prohibition is not a measure designed to give indirect protection to a national product or aimed at creating arbitrary discrimination depending on where the goods are produced. [1979] E.C.R. 3795.

COMMENTARY
Henn and Darby illustrates the general requirement of Article 36 that a measure must be necessary, but must not involve arbitrary discrimination or a disguised restriction on inter-

member trade. Contrast *Conegate Ltd. v. H.M. Customs and Excise* (Case 121/85) in which there was a lawful domestic trade in the goods in question (inflatable dolls). Seizure of dolls being imported from Germany into the United Kingdom on grounds that they were indecent and obscene was a breach of Article 30, being discriminatory on grounds of nationality.

KEY PRINCIPLE: *Restrictions on imports or exports may be justified on grounds of public policy.*

R. v. Thompson and Others (Case 7/78) 1978

United Kingdom law in force at the time prohibited the importation of gold coins and export of silver-alloy coins minted before 1947. The case turned on the distinction between whether the coins were "goods" or "means of payment". Under United Kingdom law it was illegal to melt down or destroy coins, even if they were no longer legal tender.

HELD: (ECJ) As the coins were not legal tender they were goods under Article 30. A ban on destroying such coins with a view to preventing their being melted down or destroyed in another Member State was justified on grounds of public policy under Article 36, because it stemmed from the need to protect the right to mint coinage which is traditionally regarded as involving the fundamental interests of the state. [1978] E.C.R. 2247.

COMMENTARY

"Public policy" is a translation of the French term "ordre public", (see Chapter 10, p. 86.). *R. v. Thompson* is a rare example of a successful invocation of the exception. Public policy does not cover consumer protection (*Kohl v. Ringelhan* (Case 177/83)) or economic considerations (*Cullet v. Centre Leclerc* (Case 213/83)).

KEY PRINCIPLE: *Restrictions on imports or exports may be justified by public security.*

Campus Oil v. Minister for Industry and Energy (Case 72/83) 1984

Irish law required importers of petroleum products to buy up to 35 per cent of their needs from the Irish National Petroleum Company (INPC) at fixed prices. Ireland sought to justify this requirement on both public policy and public security grounds, claiming that this was the only method by which the national refining capacity could be maintained and the products sold.

HELD: (ECJ) The measure was justified on grounds of public security rather than public policy. Maintaining a refinery enabled Ireland to enter into long-term contracts with oil producers who would ensure greater continuity of oil supplies during a crisis. [1983] E.C.R. 2727.

COMMENTARY
The ECJ accepted that a measure justified on grounds of public security might also achieve economic objectives without taking it outside Article 36.

KEY PRINCIPLE: *Restrictions on imports and exports may be justified on grounds of protection of life and health of humans, animals or plants.*

Officier van Justitie v. Kaasfabrik Eyssen B.V. (Case 53/80) 1981

A cheese producer was prosecuted in the Netherlands for using nisin, a preservative prohibited under Dutch law, in processed cheese. Nisin was a permitted ingredient in other Member States. Scientific research was divided as to the harmfulness of the additive. The cheese producer argued that the ban infringed Article 30 as it impeded imports.

HELD: (ECJ) In the absence of harmonisation, a state may protect the public by banning additives where there is genuine scientific doubt about their safety. [1981] E.C.R. 409.

COMMENTARY
(1) This decision forms part of a series of cases on the use of additives (*cf Commission v. Germany* see p. 64). In *Ministre Public v. Claude Muller* (Case 304/84) it was held that the

requirement for authorisation for specific additives is subject to the principle of proportionality; thus the process of application must be rapid and straightforward. Prior national authorisation may also be required for medical products (*Lucien Ortscheit GmbH v. Eurim-Pharm GmbH* (Case C-320/93).

(2) Parallels may be drawn with the continuing crisis over beef and BSE. Scientific evidence is inconclusive over the cause of the disease and on the steps needed to protect humans and livestock. The Commission imposed a worldwide export ban on British beef in 1996 as part of a package of measures. The United Kingdom unsuccessfully claimed interim relief against the measures in the ECJ. See *U.K. v. E.C. Commission (Re Emergency Measures to Protect Against BSE)* (Case C-180/96R). The United Kingdom's challenge to the measures continues.

KEY PRINCIPLE: *The risk to health must be real and form part of a seriously considered health policy.*

Commission v. U.K. (Case 40/82) 1982

The United Kingdom unilaterally and hastily introduced a ban on the importation of poultry meat and eggs after extensive lobbying by United Kingdom poultry producers just before Christmas 1981. The United Kingdom Government claimed that the measure was necessary under Article 36 to prevent British flocks catching a form of poultry disease known as Newcastle disease. An Article 177 reference was made.

HELD: (ECJ) The ban was not part of a health policy but was a disguised restriction on trade. Less restrictive methods would have been sufficient. The measure could not be justified on grounds of animal health under Article 36. [1982] E.C.R. 2793.

COMMENTARY

The measure appeared to be an attempt to protect United Kingdom producers from French competition. French turkey farmers later sought to recover their losses from the United Kingdom Government in *Burgoin v. MAFF* (C.A.). Although the claim was struck out they won an out of court settlement of £3.5 million.

KEY PRINCIPLE: *Restrictions on imports and exports may be justified on grounds of the protection of national treasures possessing artistic, historic or archaeological value.*

Commission v. Italy (Re Export Tax on Art Treasures) (Case 7/68)

The Italian Government imposed a tax on the export of art treasures from Italy, claiming that such a tax would be less restrictive than an export ban. The Commission brought an action in the ECJ under Article 169.

HELD: (ECJ) The measure was illegal under Article 12 (prohibition on customs duties and measures equivalent to customs duties). It could not therefore be justified under Article 36. [1968] E.C.R. 423.

COMMENTARY

In the absence of definitive case law, some guidance may be found in Regulation 3911/92 (implemented by Regulation 752/93) which seeks to impose uniform standards at borders on the export of protected cultural goods within a licensing scheme for art treasures. Directive 93/7 gives Member States the right to define their national treasures unlawfully removed abroad.

KEY PRINCIPLE: *Restrictions on imports and exports may be justified on grounds of the protection of industrial and commercial property.*

EMI Electrola v. Patricia (Case 341/87) 1989

Patricia and other record companies sought to take advantage of the fact that the copyright to the records of Cliff Richard had expired in Denmark but not in Germany by buying recordings in Denmark and importing them for resale in Germany.

HELD: (ECJ) The recordings had not been marketed by the holder of the copyright (EMI) or with his consent, even though they had been lawfully placed on the market. EMI could rely on the copyright to keep out the recordings. [1989] E.C.R. 79.

COMMENTARY

Intellectual property rights (as industrial property rights are now better known) take forms such as trademarks, copyright, patents and design rights. They usually operate at national level to provide protection for the holder of the right on a territorial basis. It follows that they may impede the free movement of goods under Articles 30 to 34. They may also infringe the competition rules under Articles 85 and 86. While Article 36 provides an express exception for industrial property rights, it states that such prohibitions must not constitute a means of arbitrary discrimination or disguised restriction on trade between Member States. Harmonisation of intellectual property rights is proceeding gradually.

9. FREE MOVEMENT OF CAPITAL

KEY PRINCIPLE: *Member States must prohibit all restrictions on the free movement of capital from July 1, 1990.*

Ministerio Fiscal v. Aldo Bordessa (Cases C-358 & 416/93) 1995

Various Spanish and Italian nationals were charged with attempting to take out of Spain more money than was permitted under exchange control laws without prior authorisation. The Spanish court made an Article 177 reference to the ECJ.

HELD: (ECJ) Article 1 of Directive 88/361 prohibiting all restrictions on the free movement of capital is directly effective from July 1, 1990. Member States may require persons crossing borders to declare their assets but may not require a prior administrative authorisation, such a requirement being disproportionate. [1995] E.C.R. I-361.

COMMENTARY
Article 67(1) of the EEC Treaty provided for free movement of capital "to the extent necessary to ensure the proper functioning of the common market". Unlike provisions on the free movement of goods, persons and services, it was not directly effective. Directive 88/361 abolished the remaining barriers to the free movement of capital under the internal market programme. Some states including Spain had an extension until the end of 1992, but this point was not pursued in *Bordessa*.

Articles 67 to 73 were repealed by the TEU and replaced by Articles 73(B) to (G), with effect from January 1, 1994.

KEY PRINCIPLE: *National laws prohibiting the export of currency without prior authorisation contravene Article 73(B) of the E.C. Treaty.*

Ministerio Fiscalo v. Emilio (Cases C-163, 164 and 250/94) 1995

Various individuals took money in excess of the permitted limits out of Spain to Turkey and Switzerland. They were prosecuted under Spanish law. An Article 177 reference was made to clarify the legal status of Article 73(B) of the E.C. Treaty.

HELD: (ECJ) Member States may not require prior authorisation before currency is exported, but may require a declaration of assets. [1995] 1 C.M.L.R. 631.

COMMENTARY

(1) *Emilio* was decided after the TEU amendments to the Treaty. It upholds the decision in *Bordessa*, demonstrating that the approach of the ECJ to interpretation of the new provisions of the E.C. Treaty follows that taken by Directive 88/361. Article 73(B) of the Treaty repeats the wording of Article 1 of the Directive. Thus Article 73(B) must be regarded as directly effective. Article 73(D) of the Treaty allows derogations on grounds of public policy and public security, provided they do not constitute an arbitrary discrimination or a disguised restriction on the free movement of capital and payments.

(2) *Emilio* extends the principle of the free movement of capital to third countries (*i.e.* non-Member States). However, note that Article 73(G) empowers the E.C. and Member States to take emergency measures to restrict capital movements to such countries.

(3) Completion of the internal market in the free movement of capital should be placed in the context of progress towards full economic and monetary union (EMU). The E.U. is increasing control over financial policy. States participating in EMU (*i.e.* not the United Kingdom, Denmark and any other states "opting out") will be unable to rely on the derogations in Article

73(D) once full EMU is achieved and the single currency (the "euro") is in operation. The third stage is due to begin on January 1, 1999.

10. FREE MOVEMENT OF WORKERS

Workers

KEY PRINCIPLE: *Freedom of movement for workers shall be secured by the end of the transitional period (December 1961) at the latest: Article 48.*

KEY PRINCIPLE: *A worker is someone who performs services for and under the direction of another in return for remuneration during a certain period of time.*

Lawrie-Blum v. Land Baden Wurttemberg (Case 66/85) 1986

Lawrie-Blum, a United Kingdom national, passed the first examination to qualify as a teacher in Germany. However, she was refused admission to the period of probationary service which must be undertaken before the second examination because she was not a German national. While Lawrie-Blum claimed that the refusal on nationality grounds infringed Article 48(2), the Land argued that a probationary teacher was not a "worker" under Article 48.

HELD: (ECJ) A trainee teacher who, under the direction and supervision of the school authorities, is undergoing a period of service in preparation for the teaching profession during which he provides services by giving lessons and receives remuneration must be regarded as a worker under Article 48(1), irrespective of the legal nature of the employment relationship. [1986] E.C.R. 2121.

COMMENTARY
(1) The meaning of "worker" must be defined in E.C., not national terms. (2) Article 48 does not give rights to E.C.

nationals working in their own countries. Thus a Surinamese mother was not entitled to join her son, a Dutch national, in the Netherlands where he was working: *Morson v. The Netherlands* (Cases 35 & 36/82) 1982.

Work and economic activity

KEY PRINCIPLE: *The rules governing the free movement of workers only apply to individuals who pursue or wish to pursue an economic activity.*

Levin v. Staatssecretaris van Justitie (Case 53/81) 1982

Mrs Levin, a United Kingdom national married to a non-E.C. national, sought a permit to reside in the Netherlands. She was refused on the ground that, as she was not gainfully employed, she could not be considered as a "favoured EEC citizen". She appealed against the decision through the Dutch courts, meanwhile working part-time as a waitress. An Article 177 reference was made.

HELD: (ECJ) The expression "worker" covers those who undertake part-time work, even where they are paid at a lower rate than the national guaranteed minimum, provided the work is genuine and not marginal or ancillary. [1982] E.C.R. 1035.

COMMENTARY
Part-time employment supplemented by public assistance was considered to be "work" in *Kempf v. Staatssecetaris van Justitie* (Case 139/85) 1986. In *Steymann v. Staatssecetaris van Justitie* (Case 196/87) 1988 a member of a religious community who received pocket money and keep was a worker because commercial activity was a genuine and inherent part of membership. Contrast with *Bettray v. Staatssecetaris van Justitie* (Case 344/87) 1989 (subsidised work carried out by a former drug addict at a rehabilitation centre was not work as it was not a genuine economic activity).

Workers' Families

KEY PRINCIPLE: *Member States shall facilitate the admission of workers' families: Article 10(2), Regulation 1612/68, provided the worker has accommodation available at a stan-*

dard considered normal for national workers in the area concerned: Article 10(3).

Commission v. Germany (Case 249/86) 1989

Germany had adopted legislation which made the renewal of
residence permits for family members conditional on their
living in housing considered normal, not only at the time of
arrival but throughout the duration of their stay. The Commission brought an action against Germany under Article 169.

HELD: (ECJ) Germany was in breach of Article 10(3) of
Regulation 1612/68. The obligation applies to the time of
arrival of each family member, after which the migrant worker
must be treated on the same basis as a worker of the state
concerned. [1989] E.C.R. 1263.

COMMENTARY

(1) Free movement of workers would be meaningless if workers could not install their families with them. Regulation 1612/
68 recognises the right of installation for workers' families
(defined as the worker's spouse, descendants under 21 and
dependent relatives in the ascendant line of the worker or his
spouse): Article 10(1). See *Surinder Singh* (Case C-370/90)
(Article 10(1) applies to family members of a worker returning
to his home state). (2) Workers and their families may remain
permanently in the state of residence, even after the death of
the worker, under Regulation 1251/70.

Spouses

KEY PRINCIPLE: *The spouse of the worker is entitled to
install himself or herself with the worker in the territory of the
state where the E.C. national is working: Article 10(1).*

Netherlands v. Reed (Case 59/85) 1986

Ms Reed lived with her partner in the Netherlands. Both were
United Kingdom nationals but only Ms Reed's partner was
employed. After living in the Netherlands for a year, Ms Reed
sought a residence permit. She claimed that social developments in the Netherlands had reached the stage where an
unmarried couple living together in a stable relationship should
be treated as husband and wife for E.C. immigration purposes.
The Dutch court made an Article 177 reference to the ECJ.

HELD: (ECJ) Social developments in a single Member State cannot affect the development of E.C. law; thus relationships outside marriage cannot entitle the individual concerned to be treated as a spouse. However, under Dutch law an alien who had a stable relationship with a Dutch national was permitted to reside in the country under certain conditions. Applying the principle of non-discrimination, an alien should be granted the same rights of residence whether cohabiting with a Dutch national or an E.C. national. [1986] E.C.R. 1283.

COMMENTARY

Ms Reed gained the right to reside in the Netherlands because there was a Dutch law giving residence rights to aliens in specific circumstances which, under Article 7 EEC was extended to her. The decision does not mean that cohabitees in general may acquire the same residence rights as a spouse.

KEY PRINCIPLE: *Separation does not dissolve the marital relationship for the purpose of E.C. residence rights.*

Diatta v. Land Berlin (Case 267/83) 1985

A woman of Senegalese nationality married a French national. The couple lived in Germany where the husband was employed. After a year they separated with the intention of becoming divorced. After Mrs Diatta's temporary residence permit expired she applied for an extension. The application was refused on the ground that, as she no longer lived with her husband, she was not a family member of an E.C. national.

HELD: (ECJ) Article 10(3) does not imply that the family must live under the same roof permanently. The marital relationship cannot be regarded as dissolved so long as it has not been terminated by the competent authority. [1985] E.C.R. 567.

COMMENTARY

In a decision which has been much criticised the House of Lords attempted to apply *Diatta* in *R. v. Secretary of State for the Home Department, ex p. Sandhu* (1985) (H.L.). Sandhu, an Indian national, married a German woman. The couple moved to the United Kingdom where a son was born. The marriage broke down, after which Mrs Sandhu and the child moved to Germany. Sandhu visited his family in Germany, but was denied re-entry to the United Kingdom on the ground that his residence rights had ended when his wife left the United Kingdom. The House of Lords considered that the position was covered by *Diatta*, refused to make an Article 177 reference and upheld the decision of the immigration authorities to deny entry. In failing to make an Article 177 reference the opportunity was lost for further clarification by the ECJ of the position of separated spouses.

Rights of Entry

KEY PRINCIPLE: *Workers who are E.C. nationals and their families are entitled, on production of a passport or valid identity card, to enter the territory of other Member States in order to work: Article 3, Directive 68/360.*

Procureur du Roi v. Royer (Case 48/75)

R, a French national with a conviction for procuring, was prosecuted with (and later convicted of) illegal entry into Belgium. R had not complied with administrative formalities on entry into Belgium where his wife ran a dance hall. He was expelled on the grounds that his personal conduct showed that he was a danger to public policy and that he had not observed the conditions for aliens. An Article 177 reference was made.

HELD: (ECJ) The right for E.C. nationals to enter the territory of another Member State covers the right to enter in search of work or to rejoin a spouse or family. Failure by a national of a Member State to complete the legal formalities on access, movement and residence, does not justify expulsion. [1976] E.C.R. 497.

COMMENTARY
(1) In *R. v. Immigration Appeal Tribunal, ex p. Antonissen* (Case C-292/89) 1991 the ECJ found that deportation of a convicted drug dealer after six months residence in the United Kingdom without finding work did not contravene E.C. law, unless the individual concerned could provide evidence that he was continuing to seek employment and had a genuine chance of finding work. (2) Involuntary unemployment is not a ground for deportation.

Equality of Treatment

KEY PRINCIPLE: *Freedom of movement entails the abolition of discrimination based on nationality between workers of Member States as regards employment, remuneration and other conditions of work and employment: Article 48(2).*

Eligibility for Employment

KEY PRINCIPLE: *E.C. nationals are entitled to take up and pursue employment in the territory of another Member State under the same conditions as the nationals of the host state: Article 1, Regulation 1612/68.*

Commission v. France (Case 167/73) 1974

The French Code du Travail Maritime specified that a proportion of the crew of merchant ships must be French nationals. While this proportion had been set at three French to one non-French crew members, the French Government claimed that it had not in practice been applied against E.C. nationals. The Commission brought enforcement proceedings against France under Article 169 for breach of Article 48 of the Treaty and Article 4 of Regulation 1612/68 (prohibition on restriction by number of percentage of E.C. nationals in a particular activity or area).

HELD: (ECJ) In failing to amend the Code in relation to E.C. nationals from other Member States, France was in breach of Article 48 of the Treaty and Article 4 of the Regulation. [1974] E.C.R. 359.

COMMENTARY
While a state may not prescribe special recruitment procedures, limit advertising or otherwise hinder the recruitment of non-nationals (Article 3, Regulation 1612/68), it may impose conditions relating to linguistic competence: *Groener v. Minister for Education* (Case 397/87) (requirement for teachers in vocational schools in Ireland to be proficient in the Irish language permissible in the light of national policy on promotion of the Irish language).

KEY PRINCIPLE: *The regulation of professional sporting activities is subject to the principle of equality.*

Union des Associations de Football v. Jean-Marc Bosman (Case C-415/93) 1995

UEFA, which regulates national football associations, had adopted two rules for implementation nationally. The first rule, incorporated into players' contracts, allowed national football clubs to impose a transfer fee when a player moved to a new club. Without a fee players could not change clubs. The second rule restricted the number of non-national players in a national club to three. Bosman, a Belgian footballer, was unable to move from a Belgian to a French club because the transfer fee was rejected. He sued the Belgian club, the Belgian national football association and UEFA, claiming that the rules infringed Article 48(2).

HELD: (ECJ) Transfer rules such as those adopted by UEFA directly affect players' access to the employment markets in other Member States and constitute an obstacle to the free movement of workers under Article 48. Rules restricting the rights of E.C. nationals to take part in professional football matches also amount to an obstacle to free movement. Such rules are covered by Article 48(2) and by Article 4 of Regulation 1612/68 (prohibition of quotas based on nationality: see p. 80 above) implementing Article 48(2). [1996] All E.R. (E.C.) 97.

COMMENTARY

Discrimination on grounds of nationality in professional and semi-professional sport contravenes both Article 48 and Article 6 of the E.C. Treaty (previously Article 7 of the EEC Treaty), the principle of non-discrimination: *Dona v. Mantero* (Case 13/76) 1976. See also *UNECTEF v. Heylens* (Case 222/86) 1987. It is, however, legitimate to restrict membership of a team on grounds of nationality for non-economic reasons (*e.g.* to represent a particular country in an international match).

Equality in Employment

KEY PRINCIPLE: *Non-national E.C. workers may not be treated differently from national workers on account of nationality in relation to conditions of employment, dismissal,* *reinstatement or re-employment: Article 7(1), Regulation 1612/68.*

Sotgiu v. Deutsche Bundespost (Case 152/73) 1974

Sotgiu was an Italian national living in Germany where he was employed by the Federal Post Office. His family remained in Italy. Under a collective wages agreement he was entitled to a separation allowance. However, the allowance was payable at a lower rate for workers whose normal residence was abroad than for those whose home was in Germany. He challenged the rate in the German courts which made an Article 177 reference.

HELD: (ECJ) A separation allowance falls within the concept of "conditions of employment and work" under Article 7(1). [1974] E.C.R. 153.

COMMENTARY
The ECJ considered in *Sotgiu* that it made no difference whether the payment was voluntary or compulsory. Once the state had decided to pay the allowance to its own nationals, it must extend the same benefit to E.C. nationals from other Member States.

Social and Tax Advantages

KEY PRINCIPLE: *Non-national E.C. workers are entitled to the same social and tax advantages as national workers: Article 7(2), Regulation 1612/68.*

Fiorini (Cristini) v. SNCF (Case 32/75) 1976

An Italian widow living in France claimed for a special fare reduction card which the French railways (SNCF) provided to the parents of large families, this concession having previously been claimed by her husband. The claim was refused because Mrs Fiorini was not a French national. She challenged the refusal in the French courts which made an Article 177 reference.

HELD: (ECJ) Article 7(2) applies to all social or tax advantages, irrespective of whether they derive from the contract of employment. As the family were entitled to remain in France (under Regulation 1251/70) they were also entitled under Article 7(2) to equal "social advantage". [1975] E.C.R. 1085.

COMMENTARY

In *Castelli v. ONPTS* (Case 261/83) (1984) a guaranteed minimum income for old people, paid to an Italian widow living with her retired son in Belgium, was held to be a "social advantage". See also *Reina v. Landeskreditbank Baden-Wurttenberg* (Case 65/81) (interest-free loan granted on child-birth by a credit institution incorporated under public law to low income families in order to stimulate the birth rate is a social advantage). (2) E.C. nationals employed or self-employed in another Member State are entitled to aggregate their periods of social security contributions in different Member States and receive benefits in whichever state they are resident: Regulation 1408/71. (3) Migrant workers are also entitled to equality of treatment in trade union membership: Article 8; and in housing (including the right to own property): Article 9, Regulation 1612/68.

Maintenance Grants and Education

KEY PRINCIPLE: *A maintenance grant to cover education is a social advantage under Article 7(2) of Regulation 1612/68.*

Lair v. University of Hanover (Case 39/86) 1988

Mrs Lair was a French national living in Germany for five years, during which time she had worked but had also been involuntarily unemployed from time to time. Having enrolled on a language course at the University of Hanover, she applied for a maintenance grant (an interest-free loan) from the German authorities. Her application was refused on the ground that she had not been employed in Germany for five years, a requirement only applied to foreign applicants. She challenged the refusal in the German courts which made an Article 177 reference.

HELD: (ECJ) (1) While Article 7 of the EEC Treaty applies to grants for access to education (*e.g.* tuition fees), it does not apply to maintenance grants. A maintenance grant is a "social advantage" under Article 7(2) of Regulation 1612/68, provided the course in question is vocational.

(2) For an immigrant to retain the status of "worker" there must be a connection between his previous career and choice of study. Member States may not lay down minimum periods of residence or employment as the concept of "E.C. worker" is a Community one which cannot be limited by national law. [1988] E.C.R. 3161.

COMMENTARY

Similar issues were raised in *Brown* (Case 197/86), decided by the ECJ on the same day as *Lair*. In *Brown* the applicant was a student with dual British-French nationality. Having been brought up in France he had been offered a place to study electrical engineering at Cambridge. To gain practical experience, Brown undertook pre-university industrial training with a firm in Scotland, such training being open only to students holding the offer of a degree place. Brown's application to the United Kingdom Government for a grant for fees and maintenance was refused as he had not lived in the United Kingdom for the required three years. The ECJ held under Article 177 that while the applicant's pre-university industrial experience gave him the status of worker, he had obtained the work only because of his university place. He was not, therefore, entitled to a grant under Regulation 1612/ 68.

KEY PRINCIPLE: *Children of migrant workers must be admitted to the host state's educational, apprenticeship and vocational training under the same conditions as the nationals of the host state: Article 12, Regulation 1612/68.*

Casagrande v. Landeshauptstadt Munchen (Case 9/74) 1974

C was the child of a deceased Italian national who had been working in Germany. His application for a monthly educational grant was rejected by the Munich authorities because the grant was payable only to German nationals, stateless persons and aliens with asylum. The Bavarian Administrative Court made an Article 177 reference to the ECJ.

HELD: (ECJ) In providing that the children of migrant workers must be admitted to educational courses under the same conditions as the nationals of the host state, Article 12 covers not only admission but also general measures to facilitate admission (*i.e.* grants and loans). [1974] E.C.R. 773.

COMMENTARY
Where a national of a Member State is employed or self-employed in another Member State, his spouse and children under 21 (or dependent) are entitled to take up any activity as an employed person in that state even if they are not E.C. nationals: Article 11, Regulation 1612/68.

Employment in the Public Service

KEY PRINCIPLE: *The principle of free movement in Article 48 does not apply to employment in the public service: Article 48(4).*

Commission v. Belgium (Re Public Employees) (Case 149/79) 1980

A wide range of posts in the public service in Belgium were advertised as reserved for Belgian nationals: posts in the National Railway Company, the National Local Railway Company, the City of Brussels and the Commune of Auderghem. The Commission brought Article 169 proceedings against Belgium which sought to invoke Article 48(4) as a defence.

HELD: (ECJ) To be covered by Article 48(4) employment must involve direct or indirect participation in the exercise of powers conferred by public law and duties designed to safeguard the general interests of the state or other public authorities. [1982] E.C.R. 1845.

COMMENTARY
(1) The distinction between posts outside and posts within the exception does not seem entirely logical. Posts outside Article 48(4) have been held by the ECJ to include nurses in public hospitals, local authority gardeners and teachers in public educational institutions, in contrast with local authority night-watchmen and architects who are within the exception. (2) In 1988 the Commission issued a notice listing occupations which should not normally be covered by the exception: public health services, teaching in state educational establishments, non-military research in public establishments and public bodies responsible for administering commercial services. Arguably, only high level posts with a particular allegiance

to the state should be covered (*e.g.* the police and the judiciary). (3) In *Commission v. Luxembourg* (Case C-473/93) 1996 the ECJ found that Luxembourg was in breach of Article 48 by restricting civil service and public sector employment in relation to teaching, health, inland transport, telecommunications, water, gas and electricity, regardless of the level of responsibility.

Derogation from the Principle of Free Movement

KEY PRINCIPLE: *Freedom of movement of workers may be restricted on grounds of public policy, public health and public security: Article 48(3).*

KEY PRINCIPLE: *Measures taken on grounds of public policy of public security shall be based exclusively on the personal conduct of the individual concerned: Article 3, Directive 64/221.*

Van Duyn v. Home Office (No.2) (Case 41/74) 1974

Ms Van Duyn, a Dutch national, sought to take up employment for the Church of Scientology in the United Kingdom. At the time the Church of Scientology was not illegal in the United Kingdom but was considered by the Government to be socially harmful. She was refused entry to take up the post on grounds that it was undesirable for anyone to enter the country to work for the Church of Scientology. Ms Van Duyn sought judicial review in the High Court which made an Article 177 reference.

HELD: (ECJ) (1) Article 48 (1) and (2) are directly effective in the national courts from the end of the transitional period (1961).
(2) Directive 64/221 is also directly effective.
(3) A Member State, in imposing restrictions on grounds of public policy, is entitled to take account, as personal conduct, of an individual's association with an organisation which the Member State considers socially harmful, even where no equivalent restriction is placed on the nationals of the host state. [1974] E.C.R. 1337.

COMMENTARY
(1) The derogations in Directive 64/221 apply not only to workers but to all categories of E.C. nationals including those exercising the right of establishment or provision of services in another Member State. "Public policy" is a translation of the French expression "ordre public" and is closer to the United Kingdom legal concept of "public order". The derogation must be strictly interpreted, although national authorities have discretion within the limits of the Treaty and secondary legislation. "Public security" is rarely invoked, but overlaps with the concept of public policy. Diseases which might endanger public health, public policy or public security are listed in an Annex to the Directive. No other diseases or disabilities may justify refusal of entry or residence permit: Article 4.
(2) *Van Duyn* appears to allow a dual standard whereby Member States may impose stricter requirements on E.C. nationals entering the country than on its own nationals. In *Adoui and Cornuaille v. Belgian State* (Joined Cases 115 & 116/81) the ECJ upheld the ruling in *Van Duyn* in the context of a refusal to grant two French prostitutes residence permits in Belgium where prostitution is not illegal. However, the Court added that in such circumstances a state must not base the exercise of its powers on assessments of conduct which would have the effect of applying an arbitrary distinction to the nationals of other Member States.

KEY PRINCIPLE: *The public policy proviso may only be invoked where there is a genuine and sufficiently serious threat to one of the fundamental interests of society.*

R. v. Bouchereau (Case 30/77) 1977
B, a French national working in the United Kingdom, was convicted of the unlawful possession of drugs in 1976. Six months earlier he had been convicted of another offence of possession and had been conditionally discharged for 12 months. The magistrates court, before recommending deportation, made an Article 177 reference to clarify the meaning of "public policy".

HELD: (ECJ) (1) A recommendation to deport is a measure under Article 3 of the Directive.
(2) Previous criminal convictions may only be taken into

account where they provide evidence of personal conduct amounting to a present threat.

(3) Recourse to the concept of public policy presupposes the existence of a genuine and sufficiently serious threat to the requirements of public policy affecting one of the fundamental interests of society. [1977] E.C.R. 1999.

COMMENTARY

(1) The threat must derive from the conduct of the individual in question and is not to discourage others. In *Bonsignore v. Oberstadtdirektor der Stadt Koln* (Case 67/74) 1975, an Italian national living in Germany accidentally shot dead his brother. He was convicted but no sentence was imposed. B appealed against his deportation order to the local administrative court which made an Article 177 reference. *Held*: (ECJ) deportation may not be ordered for reasons of a general preventive nature. Failure to observe administrative formalities does not provide grounds for deportation: *Royer* (Case 48/75) (see p. 79). (2) Procedural rights covering the right of re-entry, the requirement to specify the grounds for decision and entitlement to remedies are also provided by Directive 64/221.

KEY PRINCIPLE: *A Member State may not impose territorial restrictions on residence on a national from another Member State except in circumstances where such prohibitions may be imposed on its own nationals.*

Rutili v. Minister of the Interior (Case 36/75) 1975

R, an Italian national and trade union activist, was required by the French authorities to reside in specified regions in France. He sought annulment of the decision on residence before the French courts which made an Article 177 reference to the ECJ.

HELD: (ECJ) Measures restricting the right of residence which are limited to part of the national territory may not be imposed on E.C. nationals from other Member States except where they could also be applied to nationals of the state concerned. [1975] E.C.R. 1219.

COMMENTARY
The ECJ in *Rutili* describes Directive 64/221 (Articles 2 and 3) as a manifestation of the principle in the European Convention of Human Rights that no restrictions in the interest of national security or public safety shall be placed on rights secured by the Convention other than those which are necessary to protect those interests in a democratic society.

11. RIGHT OF ESTABLISHMENT AND FREEDOM TO PROVIDE SERVICES

The right of establishment

KEY PRINCIPLE: *Restrictions on the freedom of establishment of nationals of a Member State in the territory of another Member State shall be abolished by progressive stages by the end of the transitional period: Article 52 (1).*

Reyners v. Belgian State (Case 2/74) 1974

Reyners was a Dutch national living in Belgium where he wished to be admitted to practise the profession of "avocat", having gained the appropriate academic qualification. He was prevented by a requirement that only Belgian nationals could be admitted. He challenged the Belgian law in the Conseil d'Etat which made an Article 177 reference to the ECJ.

HELD: (ECJ) Article 52 became directly effective by the end of the transitional period and was not dependent on the adoption of further directives under the General Programme. [1974] E.C.R. 631.

COMMENTARY
(1) The right of establishment under Article 52 entitles an E.C. national who is established in one Member State to set up a business in another state on the same conditions as a national of the state concerned. E.C. nationals may take up and pursue activities as self-employed persons and set up and manage undertakings. They may also establish an

agency, branch or subsidiary an another state. The right applies both to natural and legal persons (companies incorporated in a Member State). There is considerable overlap between the right of establishment and the provision of services: see below.

(2) The transitional period ended in December 1961. The General Programme for the aboliton of restrictions on the freedom of establishment was adopted in 1961 under Article 57 of the Treaty. In 1974 the Commission decided that further directives on the right of establishment were unnecessary. Note that it was also held in *Reyners* that the profession of advocate is not an activity connected with state authority under Article 55 and is thus not excluded from Article 52.

(3) In *Commission v. U.K.* (Case C-246/89) (see Chapter 1, p. 5) United Kingdom requirements based on nationality and domicile for registration of fishing vessels were discriminatory. They infringed Articles 52 and 59 (freedom to provide services) and resulted in an order against the United Kingdom government (in *Factortame III* (Case C-48/93) to compensate the Spanish fishermen who suffered financial loss.

KEY PRINCIPLE: *Even where there is no discrimination on grounds of nationality, national requirements on qualifications may hinder the right of establishment under Article 52.*

Vlassopoulou v. Ministerium for Justiz, Bundes-und Europaangelegenheiten Baden-Wurttemberg (Case C-340/89)

V, a Greek lawyer and member of the Athens Bar, sought admission as a lawyer in Germany. She challenged the German demand to examine her qualifications for comparison with national requirements.

HELD: (ECJ) A Member State may require the examination of an individual's qualifications from another Member State before admission to the legal profession to determine the extent to which the knowledge and qualification attested by the diploma correspond to those of the host state. [1993] 2 C.M.L.R. 221.

COMMENTARY
Where a diploma corresponds only partially, the individual may be required to prove that he or she has acquired the

necessary knowledge and qualifications. Contrast *Vlassopoulou* with *Thieffry v. Conseil de L'Ordre des Avocats a la Cour de Paris* (Case 71/76) in which a Belgian lawyer with academic qualifications recognised as equivalent, was refused admission to the Paris Bar because he lacked a French diploma. *Held:* (ECJ) such a requirement breached Article 52. See also *Patrick v. Ministre des Affaires Culturelles* (Case 11/77) where a United Kingdom trained architect could not be prevented from practising in France where his qualifications were recognised as equivalent.

KEY PRINCIPLE: *Rights of establishment and the provision of services may be restricted where the limitation is objectively justified in the general interest.*

Commission v. Germany (Case 205/84) 1986

German law required the providers of insurance services in the territory to be established in Germany. Prior authorisation was also required from the German authorities. The Commission brought an action against Germany in the ECJ under Article 169.

HELD: (ECJ) The requirement for the providers of insurance services to be established in Germany infringed Article 52. However, the requirement for prior authorisation was justified in so far as it protected policy holders and insured persons. [1986] E.C.R. 3755.

COMMENTARY

(1) The single market in financial services has since *Commission v. Germany* and other cases been completed with the adoption of a number of directives including measures to harmonise safeguards and standards in insurance.

(2) In *Gebhard v. Consiglio Dell' Ordine Degli Avvocati Procurator di Milano* (Case C-55/94) a German member of the Stuttgart Bar was subjected to disciplinary proceedings by the Milan Bar for practising in Italy using the title "avvocato". The ECJ in an Article 177 reference held that where national measures restrict one of the fundamental freedoms, they must be:

(a) non-discriminatory;
(b) justified by imperative requirements in the general interest;

(c) suitable for attaining the objective;
(d) not disproportionate.

The provision of services

Qualifications and residential requirements

KEY PRINCIPLE: *Restrictions on the freedom to provide services shall be progressively abolished during the transitional period for E.C. nationals established in one Member State and providing services in another Member State: Article 59.*

Commission v. Greece (Case C-198/89) 1991

Greek law required tourist guides accompanying tour groups from other Member States to hold a licence granted only to diploma holders who had undertaken specific training. (A separate requirement for specialised professional guides covered visits to museums and other monuments.) The Commission brought an action in the ECJ under Article 169 against Greece on the basis that the requirement for a licence infringed Article 59.

HELD: (ECJ) While the general interest in the proper appreciation of the artistic and archaeological heritage of a country may justify a restriction on the provision of services, the requirement for a licence had a disproportionate effect. (It reduced the number of available tour guides, particularly those speaking the language of the tour group.) The measure infringed Article 59. [1991] E.C.R. I-727.

COMMENTARY
(1) A similar requirement in relation to tourist guides in France was also found to be disproportionate in *Commission v. France* (Case C-154/89).
(2) Many cases on Article 59 concern national requirements for professional qualifications which, without harmonisation or recognition, may severely limit both establishment and the provision of services. Directive 89/48 provides for the recognition of qualifications requiring higher education diplomas of three years or more duration where education or training is substantially the same. Where there is a substantial differ-

ence, an aptitude test or period of adaptation may be required by the host state. The principle is extended to qualifications of less than three years by Directive 92/51.

KEY PRINCIPLE: *Restrictions such as a residential requirement may infringe Articles 52 and 59 unless they are necessary to observe professional rules of conduct.*

Van Binsbergen v. Bestuur van de Bedrifsveerniging voor de Metaalnijverheied (Case 33/74) 1974

Kortman, the legal adviser of Van B, was told that he could no longer represent his client before the Dutch courts when he moved from the Netherlands to Belgium. An Article 177 reference was made.

HELD: (ECJ) Article 59 is directly effective from the end of the transitional period. A residence requirement contravenes Article 59 unless it is objectively justified by the need to observe professional rules of conduct. [1974] E.C.R. 1299.

COMMENTARY
(1) The line of case law dealing with the possible objective justification of residential and other nationally based requirements, as in *Commission v. Germany* (see above), is analagous to the "rule of reason" in *Cassis de Dijon*. (See p. 64).
(2) Lawyers seeking to provide services in other Member States are covered by Directive 77/249, but there is no equivalent directive on establishment.

KEY PRINCIPLE: *Where qualifications are not covered by a specific directive and are outside Directives 89/48 and 92/51, the basic rules on recognition and equivalence continue to apply.*

Colegio Oficial de Agentes de la Propriedad Immobiliara v. Aguirre, Newman and others (Case C-104/91) 1992

Newman, a United Kingdom national and member of the Royal Institute of Chartered Surveyors, applied for membership of the Colegio, the body which regulated estate agency in

Spain. Having received no response, he began practising as an
estate agent in Spain. He was prosecuted by the Spanish
authorities in 1991 before the implementation date of Directive
89/48 on the mutual recognition of qualifications. An Article
177 reference was made.

HELD: (ECJ) In the absence of harmonisation measures,
Member States may specify the knowledge and qualifications
needed to pursue a profession and to require the production of
a diploma certifying the status of the holder's qualifications.
[1992] E.C.R. I-3003.

COMMENTARY
In the circumstances, Spain could carry out a comparative
examination of knowledge and qualifications. Full reasons for
a refusal to recognise qualifications must be given.

KEY PRINCIPLE: *Where measures have been adopted to
harmonise professional qualifications, national authorities
must examine the experience of an applicant to a regulated
profession to evaluate post qualification experience.*

Haim v. Kassenzahnarttliche Vereinigun Nordhein (Case C-319/92) 1994
H was an Italian national who had qualified as a dentist in
Turkey. He had practised in both Turkey and Belgium before
seeking to practise in Germany. Professional qualifications for
dentistry had been harmonised in an E.C. directive. The German authorities refused his application on the basis that he
lacked the necessary qualifications. H challenged the refusal in
the German courts, claiming that it infinged Article 52. A
reference to the ECJ was made under Article 177.

HELD: (ECJ) Failure to examine post-qualification experience may infringe Article 52 where the effect is to hinder E.C.
nationals from exercising the right of establishment. [1994]
E.C.R. I-425.

COMMENTARY
After harmonisation, Member States should consider
relevant post-qualification experience as well as formal
qualifications.

Provision of non-professional services

KEY PRINCIPLE: *Article 59 applies to services offered for remuneration across national borders. The right to provide services may only be restricted where there are overriding reasons and the restriction is not disproportionate.*

H.M. Customs and Excise v. Schindler (Case C-275/92) 1992

S, acting on behalf of four local state lotteries in Germany, sent letters from the Netherlands to the United Kingdom inviting the recipients to take part in the lotteries. They enabled purchasers to participate in the lottery on payment of the price of the ticket and were offered outside the state in which the operators were established. The Customs and Excise authorities seized the letters on the grounds that they infringed United Kingdom legislation on lotteries and gambling. Schindler challenged the seizure in the United Kingdom courts. An Article 177 reference was made.

HELD: (ECJ) The letters were not goods but were services under Article 59. While legislation such as that applicable in the United Kingdom restricted the provision of services, it was justified in the public interest and was not disproportionate. [1994] E.C.R. I-1039.

Alpine Investment B.V. v. Minister van Financien (Case C-384/93) 1995

Dutch law prohibited "cold calling" (*i.e.* telephone contact by firms to potential customers without their prior written consent). The restriction applied to all firms established in the Netherlands, regardless of the location of their clients. Alpine Investments, a provider of financial services, was thus unable to canvass potential customers in the United Kingdom.

HELD: (ECJ) While such a measure in principle infringed Article 59 it was justified to protect consumers and the Dutch securities market. It was not disproportionate. [1995] E.C.R. I-1141.

COMMENTARY

(1) The ECJ distinguished *Alpine Investments* from *Keck and Mithouard*. (See Chapter 9.) A restriction on cold calling,

unlike legislation on selling arrangements, directly affects access to the market in other Member States and can hinder intra-E.C. trade.

(2) See also *Säger v. Dennenmeyer* (Case C-76/90) in which a United Kingdom company was prevented from exercising patent renewal services in Germany by national legislation. *Held* (ECJ): Although the rules did not discriminate on grounds of nationality, they hindered D's access to the German market and were disproportionate.

Freedom to receive services

KEY PRINCIPLE: *Article 59 covers the freedom to receive as well as to provide services.*

Luisi and Carbone v. Ministero del Tesoro (Case 286/83) 1984

Luisi and Carbone had, independently of each other, taken money out of Italy in excess of the amount permitted under exchange control regulations to pay for medical and tourist services. An Article 177 reference was made during their prosecution under Italian law.

HELD: (ECJ) Tourists, persons receiving medical treatment and persons travelling for the purpose of education and business are covered by Article 59. [1984] E.C.R. 377.

COMMENTARY
The principle of non-discrimination (Article 6 of the E.C. Treaty, formerly Article 7 of the EEC Treaty) applies to the receipt as well as the provision of services. In *Cowan v. Tresor Public* (Case 186/87) a United Kingdom national "mugged" on the Paris Metro, claimed but was refused compensation for his injuries out of public funds. The ECJ held that as a tourist he was entitled to compensation on the basis of equal teatment. In *Commission v. Spain* (Case C-45/93) the ECJ found that charging a discriminatory entrance fee for non-nationals to enter museums infringed Article 7.

The economic element

KEY PRINCIPLE: *"Services" are normally provided for remuneration, in so far as they are not covered by other provisions on free movement of goods, persons and capital: Article 60.*

Society for the Protection of the Unborn Child (Ireland) Ltd. v. Grogan (Case C-159/90) 1991

Officers of a student association in Ireland (where abortion is illegal) had distributed information without charge about the availability of abortion services in other Member States.

HELD: (ECJ) In the absence of an economic element, the provision of information about abortion services in other Member States is outside the scope of Article 59. [1991] E.C.R. 4685.

COMMENTARY

(1) Freedom to move around the E.C. remains largely dependent on economic status, whether exercising the rights of the worker, of establishment or the provision and receipt of services. Directives have been adopted to provide residence rights for certain categories of individuals who are not economically active: Directive 90/364 (individuals and their families with sickness insurance and sufficient resources), Directive 90/365 (former employees, the self-employed and their families) and Directive 93/96 (students for the duration of their studies). Article 8 of the E.C. Treaty has introduced the category of "citizenship of the Union" for E.U. nationals, regardless of economic status. Under Article 8a, E.U. citizens have the right (subject to limitations) to reside anywhere in the E.U. This right is not fully implemented.

(2) Derogation from the principle of free movement is permissible for the non-economically active only under the same terms as for workers and the self-employed under Directive 64/221 (see Chapter 10, p. 87).

Education and vocational training

KEY PRINCIPLE: *Discrimination in access to vocational training on grounds of nationality infringes Article 6 of the E.C. Treaty (Article 7 EEC).*

Gravier v. City of Liege (Case 293/83) 1985

Gravier, a French national, had been offered a place by the Academie Royale des Beaux-Arts in Liege on a four year course to study the art of the strip cartoon. She objected to paying the "minerval", an enrolment fee payable by students who were not Belgian nationals, claiming that the payment infringed Article 7 of the EEC Treaty and Article 59 (receipt of services). An Article 177 reference was made.

HELD: (ECJ) (1) Conditions of access to vocational training are covered by the Treaty. The imposition of a fee such as the "minerval" on students who are not nationals of the host state constitutes discrimination contrary to Article 7.
(2) Any form of education which prepares for a qualification or particular profession, trade or employment, or which provides the necessary training and skills for such a profession, trade or employment is vocational training, even if the programme includes an element of general education. [1985] E.C.R. 593.

COMMENTARY
The ECJ has interpreted "vocational training" widely, to cover almost all undergraduate degrees except those intended to benefit general knowledge rather than to prepare for a profession: *Barra v. Belgium and City of Liege* (Case 309/85). In *Blaizot v. University of Liege* (Case 24/86) the ECJ held that a six year veterinary course, the first half of which was academic and the second half vocational, should be regarded as a single course of vocational training. The consequence of *Gravier* and subsequent decisions has been that E.C. nationals attending undergraduate degree courses in E.C. states other than their own can no longer be charged higher fees than home students. There is no entitlement to a grant from the host state: *Brown v. Secretary of State for Scotland* (Case 197/86) and *Lair v. University of Hanover* (Case 39/86).

12. COMPETITION LAW 1

Agreements and restrictive practices under Article 85

The prohibition

KEY PRINCIPLE: *The following are prohibited as incompatible with the common market: all agreements between under-*

takings, decisions by associations of undertakings and concerted practices which may affect trade between Member
States, and which have as their object or effect the prevention, restriction or distortion of competition within the common
market: Article 85(1).

Agreements between undertakings

KEY PRINCIPLE: *Agreements between undertakings are
prohibited.*

ACF Chemiefarma v. Commission (Case 41/ 69) 1970

Quinine producers entered into an export agreement relating
to trade with third countries and a "gentlemen's agreement" in
1962 governing the conduct of its members in the common
market. In the export agreement the parties agreed to be
bound by the gentlemen's agreement. The Commission found
that both agreements were an indivisible entity and contravened Article 85. The applicants challenged the decison in the
ECJ under Article 173.

HELD: (ECJ) Having regard to the conduct of the parties in
relation to sharing domestic markets, the fixing of common
prices, determination of sales quotas and prohibition of making
synthetic quinine, it was clear that the parties intended to be
bound by the gentlemen's agreement which amounted to a
restriction on competition contrary to Article 85. [1970]
E.C.R. 661.

COMMENTARY
(1) An agreement may be caught by Article 85 even where it is
not a legally binding contract. The *ACF Chemiefarma* (Quinine Producers) gentlemen's agreement was covered
because it could be enforced through arbitration. The agreement is an example of a horizontal agreement which seeks to
partition the E.C. on national lines.
(2) Any legal or natural person engaged in economic activity
may be regarded as an undertaking, *e.g.* an opera singer in
Re Unitel (Commission Decision, 1978).
(3) The competition rules in Articles 85 and 86 are extended to
public undertakings engaging in commercial activity by Article
90: *Italy v. Sacchi* (Case 155/73).

(4) Agreements between parent companies and subsidiaries are not regarded as agreements between undertakings where they form a single economic unit: *Viho Europe BV v. Commission* (Case T-102/92).

(5) Decisions by associations usually involve trade associations, often acting informally. Such decisions may breach Article 85.

Concerted practices

KEY PRINCIPLE: *A concerted practice arises where positive steps short of an agreement have been taken to align the activities of undertakings.*

Imperial Chemical Industries Ltd v. Commission ("Dyestuffs") (Case 48/69) 1972

ICI was one of ten undertakings which together produced about 80 per cent of the market in dyestuffs in the E.C. It was the first undertaking to announce a price rise in 1964, shortly followed by identical increases by the other dyestuff producers. Further increases took place in 1965 and 1967, again mirrored by the other producers. The Commission decided that there had been a concerted practice contrary to Article 85 and imposed fines on the undertakings. The undertakings challenged the decision under Article 173 in the ECJ, claiming that the price rises had not resulted from a concerted practice but from parallel behaviour in an oligopolistic market (*i.e.* in a market dominated by a few producers, with each producer following the "priceleader").

HELD: (ECJ) (1) From the number of producers concerned, it could *not* be said that the European dyestuffs market operated on the basis of oligopoly (dominance by a few producers). Price competition should have continued to operate, making it inconceivable that parallel pricing would occur.

(2) The general and uniform increase on the various markets could only have arisen as a result of a common intention by the undertakings to adjust prices and to avoid the risks of competition. [1972] E.C.R. 619.

COMMENTARY

(1) It is necessary to examine price rises, even where they are identical or very similar, to decide whether they reflect an

independent response to the market or evidence of a concerted practice. The ECJ in '*Dyestuffs*' considered that the
producers had eliminated uncertainty between themselves
over future behaviour and, therefore, most of the risk inherent
in independent change of conduct.

(2) The ECJ limited its stance on behaviour amounting to a
concerted practice in *Ahlström oy v. Commission* ("*Woodpulp*") (Joined Cases C-89, etc. /85), a decision arising out
of the practice of woodpulp producers of announcing maximum price rises on a quarterly basis to their customers. The
ECJ found no breach of Article 85, holding (on the facts) that
the price announcements to users constituted market behaviour which did *not* lessen each undertaking's uncertainty as
to the future attitude of its competitors.

Effect on inter-member trade

KEY PRINCIPLE: *There must be an effect on inter-member
trade.*

Societe Technique Miniere v. Maschinenbau Ulm GmbH (Case 56/65) 1966

MBU agreed to give STM exclusive distribution rights in
France of heavy earth-moving equipment on condition that
STM would not sell competing machines. The agreement
was challenged before a French court which made an Article
177 reference to the ECJ.

HELD: (ECJ) "It must be possible to foresee . . . that the
agreement in question may have an influence, direct or indirect, actual or potential, on the pattern of trade between Member States". [1966] E.C.R. 235.

COMMENTARY
(1) The ruling demonstrates the wide interpretation placed by
the ECJ in *STM v. Maschinenbau* on "effect on trade between
Member States". It means that an agreement will be covered
by the prohibition even where it relates to a single Member
State, provided there is a potential for exports to another
Member State. See *e.g. Pronuptia v. Schillgalis* (Case 161/
84) in which a franchising agreement intended to relate to a
territory within Germany was found to have a potential effect
on trade.

(2) A very different (potentially positive) effect on trade may be seen in *Publishers' Association v. Commission* (Case C-360/92P) where the ECJ overturned part of the CFI's decision to refuse exemption to the Net Book Agreements (a series of agreements between book publishers and retailers providing for certain books to be sold at fixed prices). The basis for the ECJ decision was that the CFI had failed to take proper account of the benefits to the book trade from the single language area formed by the British and Irish book markets. Soon after the ECJ decision, the Net Book Agreements collapsed due to commercial pressures.

Prevention, restriction or distortion of competition

KEY PRINCIPLE: *An agreement is prohibited if its object or effect is to prevent, restrict or distort competition.*

Consten and Grundig v. Commission (Joined Cases 56 & 58/64) 1966

The German electronics company G entered into an exclusive distribution agreement with C whereby G agreed to supply C as sole distributor in France. In return C agreed not to sell any competing products in France or to re-export Grundig products. In additon, C was granted sole use in France of G's international trade mark (GINT). UNEF, another French company, bought Grundig products in Germany where they were sold more cheaply and resold them in France. C sued UNEF in the French courts for infringement of the GINT trade mark. UNEF applied successfully to the Commission for a decision that the agreement between G and C infringed Article 85. G and C challenged the decision in the ECJ under Article 173.

HELD: (ECJ) (1) The object of the distribution agreement was to eliminate competition to the detriment of consumers.
(2) There is no need to take account of the effects of an agreement once it appears that it has as its object the prevention, restriction or distortion of competition. [1966] E.C.R. 299.

COMMENTARY
(1) The use of the GINT trade mark could not be enforced by Consten because it had the effect of partitioning the market

along national lines. (2) The ECJ decided that the list of illegal practices set out after the prohibition in Article 85(1) is illustrative rather than exhaustive. The practices include agreements to fix prices, limit production or markets, apply different conditions to equivalent transactions and impose unconnected supplementary obligation. (3) The decision in *Consten and Grundig* has been criticised because it prohibits vertical agreements (*i.e.* agreements between undertakings at different levels of distribution, in this case between producer and distributor). Vertical agreements are seen as less damaging to consumers than horizontal agreements (*i.e.* agreements between undertakings at the same level of distribution, such as a cartel between retailers). Some commentators have thus taken the view that it is not necessary to ban agreements which restrict the availability of a particular brand where there is effective inter-brand competition (*i.e.* competition between brands).

KEY PRINCIPLE: *It is not necessary to carry out a market analysis where the object of the agreement is to prevent, restrict or distort competition.*

Societe Technique Miniere v. Maschinenbau (Case 56/65) 1966

For facts, see p. 101.

HELD: (ECJ) (1) The terms "object or effect" are "disjunctive" (*i.e.* alternatives). (2) Exclusive distribution agreements do not necessarily restrict competition. [1966] E.C.R. 235.

COMMENTARY
(1) Where it is not apparent that the object of the agreement is to restrict competition, a market analysis should be carried out to determine whether the effects of the agreement infringe Article 85(1). (2) The following factors were identified in *STM* as relevant for consideration in a market analysis: (a) the market shares of the parties; (b) whether the agreement formed part of a network; (c) the nature or quantity of the products to which the agreement relates; (d) the severity of the restrictions; and (e) whether parallel imports or re-exports were prohibited.

KEY PRINCIPLE: *A distribution agreement will infringe Article 85(1) where it substantially excludes other dealers.*

Delimitis v. Henninger Vrau (Case C-234/89) 1991

A tenant challenged the requirement under a beer supply agreement to buy all the beer for his bar from his landlord, claiming that it infringed Article 85(1). An Article 177 reference was made.

HELD: (ECJ) (1) A full analysis was needed to establish whether so many outlets were tied to brewers that there were insufficient independent outlets to provide a viable market for a new brewer to supply. (2) A selective distribution system does not infringe Article 85(1) where resellers are chosen on the basis of objective criteria of a qualitative nature and the conditions for the application of such criteria are laid down for all potential resellers. [1991] E.C.R. I-935.

COMMENTARY

(1) *Delimitis* repeats the formula previously adopted by the ECJ in *Metro-Grossmarkte GmbH v. Commission* (Case 326/76) in relation to selective distribution systems. The approach of the ECJ reflects the concept, borrowed from the United States' anti-trust law, known as the "rule of reason". Applying the rule of reason, agreements which are not automatically illegal are considered within the context of the market to decide whether they are anti-competitive. Article 85(3) recognises this pragmatic approach by providing for exemption from the consequences of illegality under Article 85(2): see p. 106 below. Negative clearance may be granted by the Commission where the agreement does not infringe Article 85(1). (2) Other examples of a "rule of reason" approach include: (a) *Remia and Nutricia v. Commission* (Case 42/84): restrictive terms in the sale of a business did not infringe Article 85(1) if necessary to give effect to the sale; and (b) *Pronuptia v. Schillgallis* (Case 161/84): restrictive clauses in franchise agreements did not breach Article 85(1) if necessary to ensure the identity of the franchiser's network or to prevent know-how being transferred to competitors.

Within the common market

KEY PRINCIPLE: *Anti-competitive agreements are covered by Article 85(1) if they are between undertakings situated within the E.C. or between undertakings situated outside the E.C., where the effects of the agreement are felt within the E.C.*

ICI v. Commission ("Dyestuffs") (Case 48/69) 1972

For facts see p. 100. Several of the undertakings engaged in concerted practices over price increases were based outside the E.C., in Switzerland and in the United Kingdom (prior to membership).

HELD: (ECJ) Because the effects of their practices were felt within the E.C., the undertakings were liable for breaches of Article 85(1). The United Kingdom parent company, ICI (U.K.) Ltd, was liable for the breaches of its Dutch subsidiary.

COMMENTARY

(1) *Dyestuffs* does not represent an entirely clear statement about the "effects" doctrine, since the issues were addressed mainly in terms of liability for the acts of subsidiaries. (2) In *Ahlström Osakeyhito v. Commission ("Wood Pulp")* (Joined Cases 89 etc./85) (see p. 101) forestry undertakings in Finland, Sweden and Canada (all, at that time, outside the E.C.) challenged the Commission decision that their advance notification of price rises infringed Article 85. The ECJ held that there was a breach of Article 85 because the practices were implemented within the E.C. It was immaterial whether they had used subsidiaries, agents or branches within the Member States.

Minor Agreements

KEY PRINCIPLE: *Agreements producing a negligible effect on trade do not infringe Article 85(1).*

Völk v. Vervaecke (Case 5/69)

Völk, a producer of washing machines with about 0.2 to 0.5 per cent of the market in Germany and an even smaller market share in Belgium and Luxembourg, entered on agreement with

Vervaecke. Under the agreement Vervaecke, a Dutch distributor of electrical products, was given exclusive rights to distribute Völk's products in Belgium and Luxembourg, with a further ban on parallel imports.

HELD: (ECJ) There was no appreciable effect on competition and therefore no breach of Article 85(1). [1969] E.C.R. 295.

COMMENTARY
The Notice on Minor Agreements 1986 provides that agreements, whose effects on trade or competition are considered by the Commission to be negligible, are outside Article 85(1). Such agreements will be outside the prohibition if the share of production and distribution of the participating undertakings does not exceed 5 per cent of the total market for such goods or services, and the aggregate annual turnover of the undertakings does not exceed ECU 200 million. It should be noted that, as notices are not legally binding, the Commission may act in relation to an agreement covered by the Notice (although it is unlikely to do so).

Illegality

KEY PRINCIPLE: *Any agreements or decisions prohibited under Article 85(1) are automatically void: Article 85(2).*

Consten and Grundig v. Commission (Joined Cases 56 & 58/64) 1966
For facts, see p. 102.

HELD: (ECJ) Only the parts of the agreement which restricted competition were void (*i.e.* those relating to restrictions on parallel importation of goods).

COMMENTARY
The decision in *Consten and Grundig* illustrates that the application of Article 85(2) need not lead to the invalidity of the entire agreement (contrary to the earlier decision by the Commission).

Exemptions

KEY PRINCIPLE: *The prohibition under Article 85(1) may be*

*declared inapplicable by the Commission where two positive
and two negative conditions are satisfied: Article 85(3).*

KEY PRINCIPLE: *For an exemption to be granted the agreement must contribute to improving production or distribution of goods, or to promoting technical or economic progress.*

Re Vacuum Interrupters (No. 1) 1977

AEI and R.P., both competing producers of heavy electrical equipment in the United Kingdom entered into a joint venture. They agreed to develop, make and sell vacuum interrupters (a form of circuit breaker) through a jointly owned subsidiary known as Vacuum Interrupters Ltd (VIL). The parties also agreed that VIL would make the interrupters but not the switchgear, that the parties would not compete with VIL, and that they would obtain all their interrupters from VIL.

HELD: (Commission) (1) As AEI and R.P. were potential competitors in the vacuum interrupter field in the E.C., their agreement brought the possibility of competition to an end. (2) The agreement facilitated the development, manufacture and sale of an efficient product as a result of the sharing of risks, to the advantage of consumers. (3) Exemption was granted under Article 85(3). [1977] 1 C.M.L.R. D.67.

COMMENTARY

(1) The *Vacuum Interrupters* decision illustrates the process by which undertakings whose agreement otherwise breaches Article 85(1) may notify the Commission to seek exemption. The full procedure for notification is set out in Regulation 17/62. Notification is a voluntary procedure. If the Commission decides not to grant an exemption it may impose fines. These may be heavy: see Chapter 13. (2) The four conditions often overlap, as in *Prym/Beka* (Commission Decision 1973), a specialisation agreement in which one party agreed to stop making needles and agreed to buy all its needles from the other party, leading to production improvements and a reduction in price. (3) An example of an agreement which improves distribution may be found in *Delimitis v. Henninger Brau* (Case C-234/89): see p. 104. (4) Promotion of technical or economic progress may be seen in many research and development agreements.

KEY PRINCIPLE: *The agreement must allow consumers a fair share of the resulting benefit.*

ACEC/ Berliet 1968

Two undertakings entered into an agreement to develop and market a bus with a new type of electrical transmission system designed by one of the parties.

HELD: (Commission) There would be a benefit to consumers, identified as the "middlemen" in a commercial transaction, in this case, the operators of bus companies. The exemption was granted. [1968] C.M.L.R. D.35.

COMMENTARY
The term "consumers" has been taken to include persons at an intermediate stage in the marketing process, rather than merely the ultimate purchaser. The "benefit" will often, though not always, involve a reduction in price. Sometimes, it will mean the availability of a new product.

KEY PRINCIPLE: *The agreement must not impose any restriction which are not indispensible.*

Consten and Grundig v. Commission (Joined Cases 56 & 58/64)

For facts, see p. 102.

HELD: (ECJ) The use of the GINT trademark in France was not required by the agreement. That part of the agreement was void.

COMMENTARY
It is possible to sever an illegal part of an agreement where the rest is valid.

KEY PRINCIPLE: *There must be no elimination of competition.*

Re Vacuum Interrupters (No.1) 1977

For facts, see p. 107.

HELD: (ECJ) As there was considerable competition between brands, the agreement did not eliminate competition.

COMMENTARY
See also *Van Landewyck v. Commission* (Joined Cases 209, etc./78) in which the undertakings in question controlled over 80 per cent of the cigarette market in Belgium. As a result, their application for exemption failed.

KEY PRINCIPLE: *Comfort letters are not legally binding.*

Lancôme v. ETOS (Case 99/79) 1980
The parties had notified a selective distribution system for perfumes to the Commission. While no formal decision had been issued, a "comfort letter" had been received stating that the system was not regarded as breaching Article 85(1). A number of retailers whom the perfumer manufacturers had refused to supply challenged the system under Article 85(1) in the French courts. An Article 177 reference was made.

HELD: (ECJ) (1) Comfort letters are administrative letters outside the structure of the Treaty; they do not bind national courts and cannot be regarded as decisions capable of annulment under Article 173. (2) Such agreements may infringe Article 85(1) where the test for admission to the selective distribution system is quantitative rather than qualitative (*i.e.* based on limiting the number of dealers rather than on objective criteria). (3) The Commission has issued a number of block (or group) exemptions to cover commonly occurring commercial practices. Where an agreement is covered by a block exemption there is no need to notify the Commission as the agreement has full validity under Article 85(3). Block exemption regulations have been issued in areas including exclusive distribution, exclusive purchasing, research and development, specialisation and franchising. Most specify maximum turnover limits. If the undertakings' turnover exceeds the limit it is not covered by the block exemption and will require an individual exemption to ensure validity. [1980] E.C.R. 2511.

13. COMPETITION LAW 2

Abuse of a dominant position under Article 86

KEY PRINCIPLE: *Any abuse by one or more undertakings of a dominant position within the common market or in a substantial part of it shall be prohibited under Article 86 as incompatible with the common market in so far as it may affect trade between Member States.*

Dominance

KEY PRINCIPLE: *Dominance results from a position of economic strength which enables an undertaking to act independently of its competitors and consumers.*

Hoffman-La Roche v. Commission ("Vitamins") (Case 85/76) 1979

H-LR held the following market shares in relation to vitamins: A—47 per cent; B2—86 per cent; B3—64 per cent; B6—95 per cent; C—68 per cent; E—70 per cent and H—95 per cent, with 65 per cent of the worldwide market for vitamins in 1974.

HELD: (ECJ) (1) H-LR could be presumed to be dominant in all vitamin markets except Vitamin A. Dominance could be shown in relation to A, as H-LR held substantially more of the market than the nearest competitor.
(2) "The existence of a dominant position may derive from several factors which, taken separately, are not necessarily determinative but among those factors a highly important one is the existence of a very large market share". [1979] E.C.R. 461.

COMMENTARY
(1) Size and turnover alone do not establish dominance. Other relevant factors identified by the ECJ include the absence of a significant competitor and the extent to which the sales network is developed.

(2) As the case law of the ECJ developed it became clear that dominance is a legal rather than an exclusively economic policy. It is established by carrying out an analysis of the relevant product, geographical and (where appropriate) temporal or seasonal markets.

(3) Note that to prove a breach of Article 86, it is not enough merely to establish dominance. There must also be abuse of a dominant position.

The product market

KEY PRINCIPLE: *It is essential to identify the product market correctly before a breach of Article 86 may be established.*

Europemballage Corporation and Continental Can Co. Inc. v. Commission ("Continental Can") (Case 6/72) 1975

Continental Can Co. Inc. (CC) were major producers of metal packages. In 1969 they took over a German company, Schmalbach (S). In 1970 CC agreed through its subsidiary, Europemballage, to acquire a majority holding in a Dutch company, Thomassen (T). At the time of the takeover of T, S and T were not in competition, although they were operating in adjacent geographical areas and were both making metal packaging. The Commission investigated the takeover of T, responsibility for which was imputed to CC by the enterprise entity concept (see Chapter 12, p. 100). The Commission decided that CC, through its holding in S, was dominant on the market for metal packaging for fish and meat and for metal closures for glass containers. It also found that the purchase of T amounted to an abuse of that position. CC and E challenged the decision under Article 173.

HELD: (ECJ) The Commission had failed to identify the relevant product market and had not given reasons for its decision. The decision was annulled. [1975] E.C.R. 495.

COMMENTARY
(1) While agreeing in principle that a takeover such as CC's acquisition of T could be a breach of Article 86, the ECJ in *Continental Can* made it clear that the Commission's failure to take sufficient account of the relevant product market was a ground for annulment. The Commission should have analysed

the undertaking's market power by defining the relevant market and then assessing the extent of dominance within that market. While there had been some consideration of possible substitutes on the demand side (meat and fish suppliers using plastic containers) it had not considered substitutes on the supply side (packaging manufacturers making alternative containers).

(2) Two key factors may be identified when identifying the product market: cross-elasticity of demand and cross-elasticity of supply (availability of demand/supply substitutes).

(3) Korah (in *E.C. Competition Law and Practice*, 5th ed., p. 70) points out that the Commission's approach in *Continental Can* follows the German practice of using a test based on demand substitution to define the market. (The test entails considering which undertaking is accused, which products are involved, who are the customers and what alternatives are open to those customers.) In recent judgments the ECJ has focused more closely on cross-elasticity of substitutes on both the supply and demand sides, as in its judgment in *Continental Can*.

KEY PRINCIPLE: *The product market should be defined by reference to product substitution, i.e. whether it is possible to interchange another product regarded by customers as identical.*

United Brands v. Commission (Case 22/76) 1978

The Commission issued a decision that United Brands had infringed Article 86 in the marketing in the E.C. of bananas grown by themselves. It considered that there was a separate market for bananas, which were not interchangeable with other fruit. United Brands challenged the decision in the ECJ on the basis that it did not hold a dominant position in the market, claiming that the relevant product market was fresh fruit and not bananas.

HELD: (ECJ) The banana has special characteristics (*e.g.* taste, softness, ease of handling) which make it very suitable for the very young, old and sick. There is little substitutability between bananas and other fruit. The banana market is a distinct market, separate from other fruits. [1978] E.C.R. 207.

COMMENTARY

The product market defined in *United Brands* was fairly narrow and related to the substitutability from the demand side. An even more limited product market was identified in *Hugin-Kassaregister A.B. v. Commission* (Case 22/78): spare parts to repair cash registers made by Hugin. See also *Hoffman-La Roche* (Case 85/76) (see p. 110), in which each vitamin was found to occupy an individual product market. In some cases, it is the possibility of substitution from the supply side which is relevant. In *Tetra-Pak Rausing S.A. v. Commission* (Case 51/89) the CFI held that the makers of milk-packaging machines could not readily transfer to making aseptic packaging for UHT milk, justifying the finding that aseptic packaging was a distinct product market.

The geographical market

KEY PRINCIPLE: *It is necessary to show that dominance occurs within the common market or a substantial part of it.*

Michelin (N.V. Nederlandsche Baden-industrie Michelin) v. Commission (Case 322/81) 1983

The Commission found that there was an abuse of a dominant position arising out of the practices of the Dutch subsidiary of Michelin in the Netherlands. The Michelin group operated a policy of price discounts which made it difficult for their customers to obtain tyres for heavy vehicles from manufacturers competing with Michelin. The product market was identified by the Commission as tyres for heavy vehicles and the geographical market as the Netherlands, where the activities of the subsidiary were concentrated.

HELD: (ECJ) The Commission decision on the product and geographical markets was upheld and the abuse confirmed. [1983] E.C.R. 3461.

COMMENTARY

(1) The geographical market may be, but is not always, the same as the sales area of the undertaking concerned. Where the product is readily transportable (in this case, nail cartridges) it may be the whole of the E.C.: *Hilti v. Commission* (Case T-30/89). Some products may have a global market:

'*Wood Pulp*'. The territories of most of the Member States have been found to be a substantial part of the common market (*e.g.* Ireland in *RTE, BBC and ITP v. Commission* (Case C-241/91P)). The ECJ was prepared to define the geographical market very narrowly in *Corsica Ferries v. Corpo dei Piloti del Porto di Genoa* (Case C-18/93) as the Port of Genoa.

(2) It is rarely necessary to define the seasonal or temporal market. The ECJ considered seasonal factors in *United Brands* (Case 22/76) but decided that they did not influence consumer choice to a signficant degree. Temporal factors were considered but rejected in *Michelin* (Case 322/81). Issues such as the need to build a new factory or for customers to assess the suitability of a new type of tyre were held to be too long term to affect competition.

Assessing dominance

KEY PRINCIPLE: *A detailed market analysis is needed to assess dominance, taking account of the market share of the undertaking and of competitors, control of production and distribution, and financial and technical resources.*

United Brands (Case 22/76) 1978
For facts and decision, see p. 112.

COMMENTARY
Market share should be examined carefully in relation to competitors. Although the market share of United Brands was fairly low (about 40 per cent), the market was fragmented, with no competitor holding more than 16 per cent. United Brands was also identified by the ECJ as possessing superior technology to its competitors. United Brands controlled virtually all stages of production and distribution, owning the banana plantations, and controlling transportation, distribution and ripening of its brand "Chiquita". Taking all these factors into account, it was clear that United Brands was in a dominant position in the banana market in the E.C.

Abuse of a dominant position

KEY PRINCIPLE: *Dominance is not illegal. Article 86 is only infringed where a dominant position is abused.*

KEY PRINCIPLE: *Abuse may be demonstrated by practices such as charging unfair prices, discriminating between customers and refusing to supply customers.*

United Brands v. Commission (Case 22/76) 1978

For facts on dominance, see p. 112. United Brands had engaged in a range of practices which the Commission had decided were abusive including forbidding the sale of green bananas, refusing to supply a Danish wholesaler because it had engaged in an advertising campaign for a competitor (thus driving it out of business), charging customers in different Member States different prices and charging excessive prices. United Brands challenged the findings of abuse in the ECJ.

HELD: (ECJ) United Brands had engaged in abuse in relation to the ban on the sale of green bananas, the refusal to supply the Danish wholesaler and differential pricing. Abuse was not proved in relation to alleged excessive pricing.

COMMENTARY

(1) The prohibition in Article 86 is followed by a list of examples of abuse similar to those in Article 85 (imposing unfair prices or other trading conditions, limiting production, markets or technical development to the detriment of consumers, applying dissimilar conditions to equivalent transactions and imposing unnecessarily supplementary obligations). The *United Brands* decision provides examples of most types.

(2) The ECJ and various academic commentators have divided abuses into exploitative abuses (taking advantage of a dominant position by imposing harsh trading conditions such as charging differential prices) and anti-competitive abuses (activities which are not necessarily unfair but which may reduce competition such as mergers: see below). Many examples of abuse show characteristics of both types.

(3) An example of a practice which may be abusive (both exploitative and anti-competitive) is the granting of discounts. In *Hoffman-La Roche* the ECJ distinguished between loyalty and quantity discounts. *Loyalty* discounts were granted to customers on the proportion of the customer's requirement for vitamins purchased. This had a "tying" effect, compelling customers to buy from H-LR and was abusive. *Quantity* discounts were granted on the basis of volume of vitamins bought from the same firm and were legal.

(4) Export and import bans are usually considered to be abusive: *BMW Belgium v. Commission* (Joined Cases 32 etc./78) (export ban considered abusive even though there was national price control leading to particularly low prices in the country of export).

Further examples of abuse

KEY PRINCIPLE: *It is an abuse of a dominant position to refuse to supply a customer.*

RTE, BBC and ITP v. Commission (Case C-241/91 P) 1995

RTE, the BBC and the ITP refused to supply Magill, a publisher in Ireland, with information about weekly television listings for the purpose of producing an independent guide. The Commission and CFI found that the refusal was an abuse of a dominant position. A further challenge was brought by the television companies in the ECJ.

HELD: (ECJ) The ECJ accepted that weekly television listings amounted to a distinct market in which the television companies were dominant. The companies could not rely on intellectual property rights to justify refusal to supply the information, such refusal amounting to an abuse. [1995] E.C.R. I-743.

COMMENTARY
See also *Commercial Solvents* (Joined Cases 6 & 7/73) in which a dominant undertaking refused to supply a former competitor with an essential chemical, driving it out of business. This was held by the ECJ to be abusive.

KEY PRINCIPLE: *"Predatory" pricing is an abuse under Article 86.*

AKZO Chemie v. Commission (Case C-62/86) 1991

ECS, a small undertaking in the United Kingdom producing benzyl peroxide, supplied its product to customers for use as a bleach in flour refining. In 1979 it decided to widen its market and sell to users in the polymer industry. AKZO, a Dutch undertaking dominant in polymers, told ECS that it would lower its prices in the flour additive market to a level with which ECS could not compete. AKZO duly reduced its prices. The Commission found that AKZO's price reduction was "predatory" and imposed an exemplary fine. The Commission took account not only of the cost in comparison to the price, but also whether it was part of a strategy to eliminate competition, what the effects of the price reduction would be and the likely reaction of the competitor. AKZO appealed to the ECJ.

HELD: (ECJ) (1) The Commission's finding under Article 86 was upheld: AKZO's behaviour amounted to predatory pricing and was an abuse of a dominant position.
(2) Prices below average variable cost give rise to a presumption of predatory pricing. [1986] 3 C.M.L.R. 273.
(3) The amount of the fine was reduced. [1991] E.C.R. I-3359.

COMMENTARY
While price competition usually benefits the consumer, predatory pricing does not. Its aim is to drive the competitor out of business, thus reducing consumer choice. The reasoning of the ECJ in *AKZO* was followed by the Commission in *Tetra Pak II* (1992) where Tetra Pak's pricing of non-aseptic cartons was found to be predatory.

Mergers and concentrations

KEY PRINCIPLE: *Mergers and takeovers may be an abuse of a dominant position under Article 86.*

Europemballage and Continental Can v. Commission (Case 6/72) 1973
For facts and decision, see p. 111.

COMMENTARY
(1) Although the ECJ annulled the Commission's decision that the takeover of Thomassen by Europemballage was an abuse of a dominant position under Article 86 (due to inadequate definition of the market and failure to give reasons), it established in principle that Article 86 may be invoked to control mergers and takeovers.
(2) Article 86 does not provide any mechanism for notification comparable to notification under Article 85(3), making it

difficult for undertakings engaged in a merger to protect themselves in the event of a merger being considered abusive. In *BAT & Reynolds v. Commission* (Joined Cases 142 & 156/84) the ECJ raised the possibility of mergers being subject to Article 85. This decision opened up the possibility of adopting the Merger Regulation (see below) which provided for advance notification of mergers.

Control of concentrations under Regulation 4064/89

KEY PRINCIPLE: *"Concentrations" (as joint ventures such as mergers and takeovers are known under the Regulation) must be notified to the Commission if they involve the performance of functions of an autonomous entity and satisfy specified turnover limits.*

ICI/Tioxide 1990

Tioxide plc is the second largest producer of titanium dioxide (mainly used in manufacturing paint) in the world. It was jointly owned, with equal holdings by ICI and Cookson. C agreed to sell its holding to ICI, the largest manufacturer of paint in the world. As the thresholds in the Regulation were met the agreement was notified to the Commission.

HELD: (Commission) Having examined (1) the possibility of imports from outside the E.C. and (2) the positions of ICI on the paint market and Tioxide on the titanium dioxide market, no problems for competition were found. The concentration was granted clearance. [1990] O.J. C304/27.

COMMENTARY
(1) Moving from joint to sole control was found by the Commission to be a concentration.
(2) Concentrations are covered by the Regulation where the undertakings concerned have a combined worldwide turnover of at least ECU 5000 million, and at least two of the undertakings have an E.C.-wide turnover of ECU 250 million, unless each party derives two thirds of its E.C. business from a single Member State. These thresholds are due to be lowered by a new regulation from March 1, 1998. The Commission will have compelence over concentrations involving undertakings with a combined aggregate turnover

of at least ECU 2,500 million. E.C. thresholds will also be reduced.
(3) Concentrations which are not cleared are illegal; undertakings responsible for them are to be fined.

KEY PRINCIPLE: *Factors to be considered by the Commission in deciding whether to clear a concentration include the structure of the markets, the market position of the parties, competition inside and outside the E.C., barriers to entry, technical and economic progress and the interests of consumers.*

Aerospatiale/ Alexia/ De Havilland 1991

Aerospatiale, a French undertaking, and Alenia, an Italian undertaking, agreed to take over from Boeing the assets of the Canadian division of De Havilland. The proposed concentration was notified to the Commission.

HELD: (Commission) Clearance under Regulation 4064/89 was refused on the basis that the move would create a new undertaking with an overwhelmingly powerful position in the market for commuter aircraft (holding 50 per cent of the world market and 67 per cent of the E.C. market). The Commission's analysis found that the merger would be likely to have the following consequences: (a) to increase the new undertaking's market share without leading to economies of scale; (b) to cause the withdrawal of some competitors from the market; and (c) to create barriers to entry for potential competitors. [1992] 4 C.M.L.R. M.2.

COMMENTARY
(1) *Aerospatiale* is a rare example of a merger being refused clearance under Regulation 4064/89. The decision has been criticised on competition grounds without considering matters of industrial policy. This dimension may become more important in future, particularly in the light of the Employment Chapter agreed at Amsterdam in June 1997.
(2) It is not entirely clear whether the Regulation applies to joint dominance. In *Nestlé/Perrier* (1992) the Commission analysed the proposed merger between Nestlé and Perrier, the bottled mineral water producer. As a result of the transaction Nestlé would sell Perrier's water source to a competitor.

Although the merger would strengthen the high market share for bottled water already enjoyed in France by Nestlé and Perrier, the Commission decided to grant clearance on condition that Nestlé sell off eight brands of mineral water to a competitor. While Nestlé and Perrier did not appeal against the decision, a challenge was instituted by the trade unions (pending) concerned that the decision appears to imply that collective dominance is covered by Article 86.

Enforcement of the competition rules under Regulation 17/62

KEY PRINCIPLE: *Investigations into breaches of competition law under Regulation 17 may be either compulsory or voluntary.*

National Panasonic (U.K.) Ltd v. Commission (Case 136/79) 1980

Suspecting an infringement (a concerted practice) of Article 85, the Commission carried out a compulsory investigation of National Panasonic (U.K.) without warning.

HELD: (ECJ) The Commission was entitled under Article 14 of Regulation 17 to investigate without prior notice where a breach was suspected. A concerted practice was found. [1980] E.C.R. 2033.

COMMENTARY
(1) Powers of entry and search relate only to the undertaking and not to the individual. Thus, they enable the Commission to enter the business premises of an undertaking under suspicion, but not to enter the home of, say, one of the directors, even if they believe that the individual has removed papers to his home. See *Hoechst v. Commission* (Joined Cases 46 & 227/88) in which the search of the home premises of a senior member of staff was found to be illegal, being in breach of the principle of the inviolability of the home, contrary to the European Convention of Human Rights. See also *Orkem v. Commission* (Case 374/87) and *Dow Benelux N.V. v. Commission* (Case 85/87), the latter upholding the decision in *Hoechst*.
(3) Investigations may also be voluntary under Article 13.

KEY PRINCIPLE: *The ECJ must have regard to the legitimate business interests of undertakings in protection of their business secrets and must not disclose information acquired to the national authorities.*

Adams v. Commission (Case 145/83) 1985

The Commission disclosed information about Adams, an informant, to the Swiss authorities, as a result of which A was charged and convicted by the Swiss courts. (For full facts, see Chapter 6, p. 50.)

HELD; (ECJ) The Commission was liable for breach of the principle of confidentiality (although damages were reduced by A's contributory negligence).

COMMENTARY
See also *Australian Mining & Smelting Co. Ltd v. Commission* (Case 155/79): limited professional privilege applies to communications between lawyer and client.

KEY PRINCIPLE: *Where a breach of the competition rules is established the Commission may order the undertaking(s) to terminate the infringement. If the breach is substantive the Commission may impose a fine up to ECU 10 million or 10 per cent of the gross annual turnover of the group of which the undertaking forms a part.*

Musique Diffusion Francaise v. Commission (Cases 100–103/80) 1983

Pressure had been applied by the Japanese group of companies to prevent parallel imports into France as part of a selective distribution system.

HELD: (ECJ) The system was found to be in breach of Article 85 and the maximum fine based on 10 per cent of the turnover of the group of companies was imposed. [1983] E.C.R. 1825.

COMMENTARY
(1) The ECJ in *Musique Diffusion* stated that basing the penalty on group turnover was likely to be unusual. This has proved to be the case. However, there have been many instances of heavy fines being imposed, the highest so far imposed by the Commission for breach of Article 85 being on

the undertakings involved in the cement cartel: ECU 248 million (Decision of 1994, subject to appeal). A fine of ECU 75 million was imposed on Tetrapak for predatory pricing (see p. 113).
(2) Appeals (in the form of an application for judicial review under Article 173) may be made against Commission decisions to the CFI and thence to the ECJ.

KEY PRINCIPLE: *As Articles 85 and 86 are directly effective, they may be enforced in the national courts.*

Cutsforth v. Mansfield Inns 1986

C sought to rely on Article 85 in relation to a term in agreement between the tenants of tied houses and the brewer which had taken over the chain of public houses. Under the agreement the tenants would only be permitted to obtain their equipment from authorised suppliers. C, who had previously supplied gaming equipment to the public houses, was not authorised.

HELD: (H.C.) There was a serious prima facie case between the parties. An interlocutory order restraining the application of the offending term was granted. [1986] 1 C.M.L.R. 1.

COMMENTARY
(1) Although it was suggested in *Garden Cottage Foods v. Milk Marketing Board* (H.L. 1983) that damages should be available for breach of Article 86, the position was not made clear in that case. Subsequently, the *Francovich* decision (Joined Cases C-6/90 & 9/90) has established that Member States are liable in damages for breaches of E.C. law (see Chapter 1, p. 11).
(2) Although national competition authorities are empowered to administer the competition rules under Article 88, national courts should not consider cases which are already subject to proceedings before the Commission. In such circumstances, a court should suspend proceedings pending a Commission decision or make an Article 177 reference to the ECJ.

14. EQUAL PAY AND TREATMENT

Equal pay

KEY PRINCIPLE: *Member States must ensure and maintain the application of the principle that men and women receive equal pay for equal work: Article 119.*

Defrenne v. Sabena (Case 43/75) 1976
For facts, see Chapter 1, p. 7.

HELD: (ECJ) Article 119 is directly effective from the date of the judgment (April 8, 1976). [1976] E.C.R. 455.

COMMENTARY
Equal pay claims within Article 119 may be enforced against both public and private bodies as Treaty provisions are effective both vertically and horizontally. By contrast, equal treatment claims under the relevant directive may only be enforced against public bodies as directives are vertically but not horizontally effective (see p. 7 and p. 134).

KEY PRINCIPLE: *"Pay" means the ordinary basic or minimum wage or salary and any other consideration, in cash or kind, which the worker receives, directly or indirectly, in respect of his employment: Article 119.*

Worringham v. Lloyds Bank Ltd (Case 69/80)
Lloyds Bank operated two retirement schemes, one for men and one for women. Male employees under 25, but not female employees, received a notional additional sum for the purpose of calculating the level of employer contributions towards pension entitlement.

HELD: (ECJ) Even though the payment was notional and was immediately removed to the pension scheme, it was "pay" under Article 119. [1981] E.C.R. 767.

COMMENTARY
(1) The payment in *Worringham* was "pay" because it was repaid to employees leaving the scheme early and was included in gross pay to calculate other entitlements such as redundancy pay.
(2) The grant of special travel facilities to former employees was held to be "pay" in *Garland v. BREL* (Case 12/81).
(3) Contributions paid into a statutory social security scheme are not pay: *Defrenne v. Belgian State* (Case 80/70), upheld in *Barber v. GRE. (Case 262/88), unlike contributions paid into an occupational pension scheme which are covered by Article 119 (see p. 125).*

KEY PRINCIPLE: *Exclusion of part-time workers from entitlements such as sick pay may contravene Article 119 where there are more female than male part-timers.*

Rinner-Kuhn v. FWW (Case 171/88) 1989

Part-time employees whose contracts limited their work to 10 hours a week or 45 hours a month were excluded from entitlement to sick pay.

HELD: (ECJ) As more women than men worked part time, such a restriction infringed Article 119 unless it was objectively justified. [1989] E.C.R. 2743.

COMMENTARY
The ECJ rejected as inadequate the "justification" of the German Government that part-time workers were less integrated into their employment and upheld its decision in *Bilka Kaufhaus* (Case 170/84) (see p. 126).

KEY PRINCIPLE: *Article 119 and Directive 75/117 apply to part-time workers in the United Kingdom, enabling them to claim for redundancy pay on the same terms as full timers under United Kingdom law.*

R. v. Secretary of State for Employment, ex p. EOC 1994

The Equal Opportunities Commission (EOC) brought an action in the United Kingdom courts claiming that provisions for redundancy under United Kingdom law infringed Article 119 and Directive 75/117 and that the conditions governing conditions for unfair dismissal for part-time workers infringed Directive 76/207 on equal treatment (see p. 131).

HELD: (H.L.) The exclusion of part-time workers from redundancy benefits and protection against unfair dismissal infringed Article 119, Directive 75/117 and Directive 76/207 respectively. [1995] A.C. 1.

COMMENTARY
The United Kingdom has given effect to this decision, *inter alia*, by the Employment Rights Act 1996.

Occupational pensions

KEY PRINCIPLE: *Payments under occupational pensions schemes are "pay" under Article 119.*

Barber v. Guardian Royal Exchange (Case C-262/88) 1990

Mr Barber belonged to a pension fund established by his employers, Guardian Royal Exchange. The scheme was non-contributory and "contracted out" (*i.e.* a private, non-statutory scheme approved by U.K. law). Under the scheme women were entitled to receive their pension at the age of 57 years, whereas men had to wait until they were 62. In the event of redundancy women received an immediate payment at 50 and men at 55. Mr Barber was made redundant at the age of 52. He received severance pay, statutory redundancy pay and an *ex gratia* payment, but was told that he would not receive his pension until he reached pensionable age (*i.e.* 62 years). Mr Barber brought proceedings in an industrial tribunal based on the Sex Discrimination Act, claiming unlawful discrimination. (A woman in his position would have received an immediate pension.) His action initially failed but reached the Court of Appeal in appeal proceedings brought by his widow after Mr Barber's death. The Court of Appeal referred questions to the ECJ.

HELD: (ECJ) (1) A pension paid under a contracted out, private occupational scheme is "pay" under Article 119.
(2) It is a breach of Article 119 in a contracted-out scheme to impose an age condition which differs between men and

women, even where permissible under national law. To enable
national courts to identify and eliminate any discrimination
between the sexes, all elements of a remuneration package
must be transparent.
(3) Equality in pension claims may only be claimed from the
date of the judgment (May 17, 1990) except for claims initiated
before the judgment. [1990] E.C.R. I-1889.

COMMENTARY
(1) *Barber* has been an immensely important decision as it
has required occupational pension schemes to harmonise the
retirement ages for men and women.
(2) The ECJ limited the temporal effect of the judgment, as it
did in *Defrenne*. This restriction was confirmed in a protocol to
the TEU.
(4) The *Barber* decision has caused Directive 86/378 (Equal
Treatment in Occupational Pensions Schemes) to lose sig-
nificance, as most issues relating to differences between men
and women in retirement ages or pension entitlement are now
covered by Article 119.
(5) Pensions paid to the spouses of deceased employees are
within Article 119: *Ten Oever v. Stichting Bedriffspensioenfonds Voor Het Glazenwassers* (Case C-109/91).
(6) The arrangements for funding occupational pensions are
outside Article 119, thus permitting schemes to require different levels of contribution from men and women based on
actuarial factors such as life expectancy: *Neath v. Hugh Steeper* (Case C-152/91). Statutory social security schemes are
also outside Article 119: *Barber*, as are "single sex" schemes:
Coloroll Pension Trustees Ltd. v. Russell (Case C-200/91).

Direct and indirect discrimination

KEY PRINCIPLE: *Direct discrimination is illegal under Article
119. Indirect discrimination may be legal if it is objectively
justified.*

Bilka-Kaufhaus GmbH v. Weber von Hartz (Case 170/84) 1980

Part-time workers were excluded from an occupational pension
scheme unless they had been employed for 15 years. Full time
employees were not similarly restricted. As nearly all the part-
timers were female, the effects were felt disproportionally by

women. A female part-timer challenged the exclusion in the German courts which made a reference to the ECJ.

HELD: (ECJ) (1) Exclusion of part-time workers from a pension scheme infringes Article 119 where: (a) a considerably smaller proportion of the workforce is employed part-time; (b) the difference in treatment is based on sex; and (c) the exclusion is not objectively justified.

(2) A measure will be objectively justified if it corresponds to a real need on the part of the undertaking, it is appropriate to achieve the objective pursued and it is necessary. [1986] E.C.R. 110.

COMMENTARY

(1) Direct discrimination occurs where one sex is treated disadvantageously compared with the other sex. (See *Dekker v. Stichtung Vormingscentrum Voor Jonge Volwassenen* (Case C-177/88), discrimination on grounds of pregnancy was held to be direct discrimination.)

(2) Indirect discrimination involves practices which are not apparently discriminatory but which have an adverse effect which is felt disproportionately by one sex, as in the exclusion of the part-time (female) employees from the pension scheme in *Bilka-Kaufhaus*, upholding the earlier decision in *Jenkins v. Kingsgate (Clothing Productions) Ltd* (Case 96/80) (paying part-time employees, most of whom were female, less than men did not infringe Article 119 if objectively justified and not based on discrimination on grounds of sex).

(3) In the United Kingdom the House of Lords ruled in *R. v. Secretary of State for Employment, ex p. EOC* (H.L., 1994) that the requirement for part-time workers to be employed for five years (compared with two years for full-time workers) before gaining certain employment protection rights was indirect discrimination which was not objectively justified.

KEY PRINCIPLE: *Men and women have equal rights to join an occupational pension scheme under Article 119.*

Dietz v. Stichting Thuiszorg Rotterdam (Case C-435/93) 1996

Dietz was employed by the defendants part-time until November 6, 1990 when she agreed to retire early at the age of 61 years. At that time part-timers were excluded from occupational pension schemes. She claimed she would have retired later if she had known about imminent changes to the pension scheme of benefit to her. The Dutch court made a reference to the ECJ.

HELD: (ECJ) The right to join an occupational pension scheme is covered by Article 119 and can be enforced against the scheme's administrators. [1997] 1 C.M.L.R. 199.

COMMENTARY

(1) The ECJ in *Dietz* followed *Vroege v. NCIV Institut Voor Volkshuisvesting* (Case C-57/93) in placing no restrictions on the temporal effect of Article 119 in this context (cf *Barber*). However it ruled that national time limits may be invoked in relation to Article 119 provided the limits are no less favourable than those relating to comparable domestic actions.

(2) On equality of access to pension schemes, see also *Fisscher v. Voorhuis Hengelo* (Case C-128/93) where the exclusion of married women from an occupational scheme was found to infringe Article 119.

Redundancy pay

Barber v. GRE (Case C-262/88)

For facts, see p. 125, above.

HELD: (ECJ) Redundancy pay is "pay" under Article 119, whether paid under a contract of employment, by virtue of legislative provisions or on a voluntary basis.

COMMENTARY

After *Barber*, the earlier decision of the ECJ in *Burton v. British Railways Board* (Case 19/81) would appear to have little relevance. In *Burton* the ECJ held that discrimination between the sexes in terms of age of entitlement to voluntary redundancy was calculated by reference to the statutory retirement age (60 for women and 65 for men). As directive 79/7 (see p. 137) permitted Member States to exclude the statutory retirement age from equal treatment, the claim under Directive 76/207 failed. Such a claim could now be brought under Article 119. United Kingdom law permitting different statutory retirement ages for men and women was amended by the Sex Discrimination Act 1986 which made discrimination between the sexes in retirement ages illegal and by the Employment Act 1989 which provides for a single retirement age of 65 years for both sexes for redundancy benefit.

Equal work

KEY PRINCIPLE: *Equal pay for equal work means the elimination of all discrimination on grounds of sex for the same work or for work to which an equal value is attributed, with regard to all aspects and conditions of remuneration: Article 1, Directive 75/117.*

Bilka-Kaufhaus GmbH v. Webervon Hertz (Case C-170/84) 1986

For facts and decision, see p. 126, above.

COMMENTARY

(1) Directive 75/117 was adopted to clarify Article 119 and to provide a mechanism for comparing work of equal value. It does not alter the scope of Article 119: *Jenkins v. Kingsgate* (Case 96/80) (see above). Thus, all considerations applying to Article 119 also apply to Directive 75/117, including the decisions of the ECJ on direct and indirect discrimination and on objective justification (see pp. 126–128).

(2) Where men and women are engaged in the same work, as in *Bilka-Kaufhaus* and *Jenkins v. Kingsgate* (see p. 127), discrimination infringes Article 119 where it is based exclusively on the difference of sex of the worker.

(3) Where statistics show a significant difference in pay for jobs of equal value where one (in this case pharmacy) is carried out almost exclusively by men and the other (speech therapy) by women, the employer must establish that the difference is objectively justified by factors other than sex: *Enderby v. Frenchay Area Health Authority and Secretary of State for Health* (Case C-127/92).

KEY PRINCIPLE: *Equal work need not be identical work but must display a high degree of similarity.*

Macarthys Ltd. v. Smith (Case 129/79) 1981

Mrs Smith was appointed by Macarthys as a warehouse manager. She complained that she was paid less than her male predecessor, who had left four months before she took up the job. The Court of Appeal made a reference to the ECJ to clarify the meaning of Article 119 in such circumstances.

HELD: (ECJ) The principle of equal pay for equal work is not confined to situations where men and women are contemporaneously doing equal work for the same employer.

COMMENTARY
While the ECJ did not rule in *Macarthys* on the meaning of "the same work", Advocate General Caportorti submitted that it included jobs which were highly similar but not identical. There must always be a real (not hypothetical) comparator, even if that comparator is not employed at the same time.

Work of equal value

KEY PRINCIPLE: *Where a job classification scheme is used to determine pay, it must be based on the same criteria for men and women, and must exclude discrimination based on sex: Article 1(2), Directive 75/117.*

Rummler v. Dato Druck (Case 237/85) 1986
The applicant challenged the criteria under a job classification scheme, claiming that she should have been placed in a higher paid category covering heavy physical work, because packing parcels was a heavy task for her. The employer considered that the job placed only light physical demands on her. A reference was made to the ECJ.

HELD: (ECJ) (1) A job classification scheme based on strength or physical hardship does not infringe Directive 75/117 provided the system precludes discrimination on grounds of sex and that the criteria employed are objectively justified. (2) "Objectively justified" means appropriate to the tasks to be carried out and corresponding to a genuine need of the undertaking.

COMMENTARY
(1) The ECJ in *Rummler* approached the issue as one of indirect discrimination, which may be capable of objective justification. It would be discriminatory to calculate the physical effort required for a job by reference to the average characteristics of one sex. However, the applicant's subjective

experience of effort was not relevant.
(2) The criteria in a job evaluation scheme must be "transparent" (*i.e.* clearly displayed): *Handels-Og Kontorfunktionaernesforbund v. Dansk Arbejdsgivforening for Danfoss* (Case 109/89). (If the criterion of "flexibility" meant quality of work, it was neutral unless it systematically discriminated against women. If it meant adaptability to work schedules it could discriminate against women due to their family responsibilities.) Each element in a remuneration package will need separate consideration in an equal value claim. See also *Barber.* p. 125.

KEY PRINCIPLE: *Member States must provide a means of assessing equal value claims if they do not provide a job classification scheme.*

Commission v. U.K. (Re Equal Pay for Equal Work) (Case 61/81) 1982

United Kingdom law provided for equal pay for people doing "like work" or work rated as equivalent in a job evaluation scheme. Such schemes were only instituted with the agreement of the employer. The Commission brought proceedings against the United Kingdom in the ECJ under Article 169.

HELD: (ECJ) (1) Job classification is only one of several ways to determine equal value.
(2) The United Kingdom's interpretation of Directive 75/117 denies the existence of the right to equal pay for work of equal value where no classification has been made, contrary to the general scheme and provisions of the Directive. [1982] E.C.R. 2601.

COMMENTARY
Under Article 6 of the Directive Member States must take the necessary measures to ensure that the principle of equal pay is applied. Effective means must be available (not necessarily by a job classification scheme).

Equal treatment

KEY PRINCIPLE: *Men and women are entitled to be treated equally as regards access to employment, including promotion,* *and to vocational training and as regards working conditions and social security: Article 1, Equal Treatment Directive 76/207.*

KEY PRINCIPLE: *There shall be no discrimination on grounds of sex in the conditions, including selection criteria, for access to all jobs or posts, whatever the sector or branch of activity, and to all levels of the occupational hierarchy: Article 3, Directive 76/207.*

Dekker v. Stichtung Vormingscentrum Voor Jonge Volwassen Plus (Case 177/88) 1990

Ms D applied for a job at a youth training centre in the Netherlands. Although the selection committee considered Ms D to be the most suitable applicant for the post she was not offered employment because she was pregnant. (The centre's insurers had refused to reimburse sickness benefits in the event of taking on an employee known to be pregnant.) The Dutch courts referred questions to the ECJ under Article 177.

HELD: (ECJ) Discrimination based on pregnancy was direct discrimination contrary to Article 3 of Directive 76/207. [1990] E.C.R. I-3941.

COMMENTARY
(1) There was no need in *Dekker* to compare the position of men and women, since women alone may be refused employment because they are pregnant. Such a refusal is therefore direct discrimination and incapable of objective justification.
(2) By contrast, where a woman becomes ill as a complication of pregnancy and is dismissed, the ECJ has held that the dismissal is indirect discrimination and is thus capable of objective justification: *Handels-Og Kontorfunktionaerer-Nes Forbund I Denmark (Acting for Hertz) v. Dansk Arbejdsgivforening* (Case 179/88).
(3) Article 4 of the Directive applies the principle of equal treatment to vocational guidance and retraining.

KEY PRINCIPLE: *There shall be no discrimination on grounds of sex either directly or indirectly by reference in* particular to marital or family status: Article 2(1) of Directive 76/207.

KEY PRINCIPLE: *The Directive shall be without prejudice to provisions concerning the protection of women, particularly as regards pregnancy and maternity: Article 2(3).*

Webb v. EMO Air Cargo (U.K.) Ltd (Case C-32/93) 1994

This decision concerned a woman who was dismissed when she became pregnant while employed on an indefinite term during the maternity leave of another employee: see Chapter 1, p. 10. The fundamental issue was whether she was unlawfully dismissed. Ms Webb claimed that the dismissal amounted to discrimination contrary to section 1 of the Sex Discrimination Act 1975 and that the Act should be interpreted subject to the Equal Treatment Directive 76/207. The House of Lords decided to refer questions for interpretation of the Directive to the ECJ under Article 177. [1994] E.C.R. I-3567.

HELD: (ECJ) Article 2(1) read with Article 5(1) of Directive 76/207 precludes dismissal of an employee who is recruited for an unlimited term with a view, initially, to replacing another employee during the latter's maternity leave and who cannot do so because, shortly after recruitment, she herself is found to be pregnant. [1994] E.C.R. I-3567.

COMMENTARY

(1) The ECJ ruled that no comparison should be made between the situation of a woman incapable of working due to pregnancy and a man similarly incapable for medical or other reasons. Pregnancy is not a pathological condition comparable to non-availability for work on non-medical grounds (which would otherwise justify dismissal without discrimination on grounds of sex).

(2) The ruling makes it clear that dismissal of a pregnant woman recruited for an *indefinite* period cannot be justified on grounds related to her inability to fulfil a fundamental condition of her employment contract. The wording may provide a loophole allowing dismissal in circumstances where a woman becomes pregnant having been engaged for a *definite* period of time (*i.e.* as a maternity leave *replacement*). This anomaly

has been resolved in the United Kingdom by the Employment Rights Act 1996, s.99 which provides that it is automatically unfair to dismiss a woman, irrespective of her hours of work or length of service, if the reason for dismissal is that she is pregnant or for any other reason connected with her pregnancy.

(3) The House of Lords' ruling on the duty to interpret national law to accord with Directive 76/207 and its subsequent decision applying the Article 177 ruling are considered in Chapter 1, p. 10.

KEY PRINCIPLE: *Men and women must be guaranteed the same working conditions, including conditions governing dismissal: Article 5 of Directive 76/207.*

Marshall v. Southampton and South West Hampshire Area Health Authority (No.1) (Case 152/84) 1986

For facts, see Chapter 1, p. 7.

HELD: (ECJ) Article 5 of Directive 76/207 does not entitle Member States to limit the application of the equal treatment principle and may be relied upon by an individual against the state before the national courts. [1986] E.C.R. 723.

COMMENTARY

(1) Ms Marshall could rely on Article 5 of the Directive against a public body, the Area Health Authority when compelled to retire at an earlier age than her male counterparts (a practice permitted at that time in the United Kingdom under the Sex Discrimination Act 1975). The *Marshall* decision is important most notably because the ECJ confirmed that directives may have vertical but not horizontal effect.

(2) The retirement age for receiving an occupational pension is not necessarily the same as the age of entitlement to state retirement benefits. The exception in the Social Security Directive 79/7 (permitting different ages for the receipt of state pension for men and women) must be interpreted strictly so as to be inapplicable to the fixing of retirement ages under occupational pension schemes.

(3) This approach was confirmed in *Roberts v. Tate and Lyle Ltd* (Case 151/84) in relation to the fixing of different retire-

ment ages for both sexes under an early retirement scheme, held to be illegal under Article 5 of Directive 76/207.

Remedies

KEY PRINCIPLE: *Member States must introduce into their legal systems the necessary procedures and remedies to enforce the equal treatment principle: Article 6 of Directive 76/207.*

Von Colson and Kamann v. Land Nordheim Westfalen (Case 14/83) 1984

For facts, see Chapter 1, p. 8.

HELD: (ECJ) While Article 6 of the Directive does not satisfy the requirements for direct effect, Member States are obliged by the principle of effectiveness (under Article 5 of the Treaty) to interpret national law to comply with the relevant E.C. Directive. [1984] E.C.R. 1891.

COMMENTARY
(1) In the context of Article 6 of the Directive, the obligation under *Von Colson* is for national authorities to interpret implementing legislation so as to ensure that it provides for appropriate procedures and remedies.
(2) See *Marshall v. Southampton and South West Area Health Authority (No.2)* (Case C-271/91) in which the ECJ held that Article 6 was directly effective and was infringed where a Member State imposed an upper limit on compensation in relation to E.C. law. The effect of this ruling was to remove the ceiling previously applied by industrial tribunals in equal treatment claims.

Exceptions to the equal treatment principle

KEY PRINCIPLE: *Member States may exclude from the operation of the equal treatment principle, occupational activities and training where the sex of the worker is a determining factor: Article 2(2) of Directive 76/207.*

Commission v. U.K. (Re Equal Treatment of Men and Women) (Case 165/82) 1983

The Commission brought enforcement proceedings against the

United Kingdom under Article 169 in relation to the implementation of Directive 76/207. The claim contained three
main complaints: (1) no United Kingdom legislation provided
that collective and other agreements which contravened the
principle of equal treatment were void;
(2) the exclusion under section 6(3) of the Sex Discrimination
1975 Act from the equal treatment of employment in private
households or where five or fewer individuals were employed
infringed Directive 76/207;
(3) section 20 of the 1975 Act wrongly excluded midwives from
the equal treatment principle.

HELD: (ECJ) The United Kingdom was found to be in
breach of E.C. law in relation to the first two complaints, but
not the third, due to the sensitivity of the midwife/patient
relationship. [1983] E.C.R. 3431.

COMMENTARY
(1) Article 2(3) allows an exception for the protection of
women, particularly during pregnancy and maternity. This
right has been extended to cover women who adopt children,
but not men: *Commission v. Italy* (Case 163/82). A similar
distinction between the sexes was taken by the ECJ in *Hofmann v. Barmer Ersatzkasse* (Case 184/83) in which extra
maternity leave granted to mothers was not extended to
fathers, the leave recognising both the biological condition
of giving birth and the relationship between mother and child.
(2) The Pregnancy and Maternity Directive 92/85 provides for
more extensive rights for mothers than the Equal Treatment
Directive 76/207.

Equal opportunities and positive discrimination

KEY PRINCIPLE: *Measures may be taken to provide equal
opportunities for men and women: Article 2(4) of Directive 76/
207.*

Kalancke v. Frei Hanseatadt Bremen (Case C-450/93) 1995

German Law operated a rule requiring the appointment of the
female applicant for a job in the event of applicants being
equally qualified in areas where women were under-repre-
sented. Mr Kalancke, a landscape gardener with the Bremen

Parks Department, claimed that he had been refused promotion in favour of an equally qualified female applicant. The German court made an Article 177 reference to the ECJ.

HELD: (ECJ) Article 2(4) of Directive 76/207 permits measures giving a specific advantage to women with a view to improving their ability to compete on the labour market and to pursue a career on an equal footing with men. It does not permit "absolute and unconditional priority" to be given to women. [1996] 1 C.M.L.R. 175.

COMMENTARY
Kalancke established that positive discrimination in favour of women is illegal under E.C. law.

Equal treatment in social security

KEY PRINCIPLE: *Men and women should be treated equally in matters of social security: Article 1 of Directive 79/7 on equal treatment in matters of social security.*

KEY PRINCIPLE: *The equal treatment principle applies to the working population, defined as "self–employed persons, workers and self-employed persons whose activity employment is interrupted by illness, accident or involuntary unemployment and persons seeking employment—and to retired or invalided workers and self–employed persons": Article 2 of Directive 79/7.*

Drake v. Chief Adjudication Officer (Case 150/85) 1986
The applicant gave up her job to care for a disabled mother. An Article 177 reference was made to clarify the scope of Article 2 of the Directive.

HELD: (ECJ) Article 2 covers all benefits designed to maintain income where any of the risks specified in the Directive have been incurred.[1986] E.C.R. 1995.

COMMENTARY
(1) Article 3 of the Directive (providing that the equal treatment principle applies to statutory schemes to protect against sickness, old age, etc., and social assistance schemes set up

to supplement or replace statutory schemes) has been held to apply to schemes exempting persons of pensionable age from prescription charges: *R. v. Secretary of State for Health, ex p. Richardsons* (Case C-137/94). Housing benefit was not, however, covered: *R. v. Secretary of State for Social Security, ex p. Smithson* (Case C-243/90) because the benefit was not directly and effectively linked to one of the risks in Article 3(1). Similar reasoning was employed by the ECJ in *Atkins v. Wrekin District Council* (Case C-228/94) in which a 63-year-old male was refused public transport concessions which were available to women at 60. The concession was held to be outside Article 3(1).

(2) The equal treatment principle has also been extended to cover occupational pension schemes (Directive 86/378) and self-employment (Directive 86/613). Directive 86/378, currently under review, has largely been superseded by the *Barber* decision that pensions paid under occupational pension schemes are "pay" under Article 119: see p. 125.

INDEX

ABORTION SERVICES,
    freedom to provide, 96–97
    misuse of Article 177 procedure,
    57
ABUSE OF DOMINANT POSITION. *See*
    COMPETITION LAW
AGREEMENT ON SOCIAL POLICY. *See*
    SOCIAL CHAPTER
ALCOHOLIC DRINKS,
    discriminatory taxation, 60–61
    mutual recognition, application
    of principle of, 63–64
AMSTERDAM TREATY,
    finalisation of, 2
ANIMALS,
    protection of life and health of,
    70–71
ANNULMENT PROCEEDINGS,
    Article 173, under, 35–44
    fundamental rights and general
    principles, protection of, 21
APPRENTICESHIP,
    children of migrant workers,
    84–85
ARTICLE 5,
    Member States' obligations
    under, 28–29
ARTICLE 30,
    measure having equivalent
    effect, 61–62
    quantitative restrictions under,
    61–67
ARTICLE 34,
    exports, restrictions on, 67–68
ARTICLE 86,
    abuse of dominant position
    under, 110–122
ARTICLE 93(2),
    illegal state aid, action on, 33–34
ARTICLE 169,
    actions under, 29–30
    force majeure no defence to action
    under, 30–31
ARTICLE 170,
    actions between Member States
    under, 32–33

ARTICLE 173,
    action for annulment under,
    35–44
ARTICLE 175,
    action for inactivity under,
    42–43
ARTICLE 177,
    invalidity ruling under, 47–48
    misuse of procedure, 56–57
    preliminary rulings under,
    51–59
ARTICLE 184,
    indirect challenge under, 43–44
ARTICLE 225,
    expedited procedures, challenge
    to use of, 34

BINDING PRECEDENT,
    doctrine of, 56

CAPITAL,
    currency, export of, 74–75
    free movement of, 73–75
COLD CALLING,
    restriction on, 95–96
COMFORT LETTERS,
    not legally binding, 109
COMMERCIAL PROPERTY,
    imports or exports, restrictions
    on, 72–73
COMMERCIAL SECRECY,
    access to measures adopted by
    Council, 20–21
COMMISSION,
    cultural integration, promotion
    of, 19–20
    social field, promotion of co-
    operation in, 19–20
COMMON MARKET,
    establishment of, 3–4
    geographical, 113–114
COMPENSATION,
    exporters, payable to, 47
    individual, to, 46–47

COMPETITION LAW,
  abuse of dominant position,
    assessing dominance, 114
    concentrations, control of,
      118–120
    customer, refusal to supply, 116
    dominance, 110–111
    enforcement, 120–122
    examples, 116–117
    geographical market, 113–114
    mergers, 117–118
    nature of, 114–116
    predatory pricing, 116–117
    product market, 111–113
    takeovers, 117–118
  Article 85, agreements and
    restrictive practices under,
    98–109
  comfort letters, 109
  concerted practices, 99–101
  consumers allowed fair share of
    resulting benefit, 108
  distortion of competition,
    102–104
  distribution agreement, 104
  economic progress, promotion
    of, 107
  elimination of competition,
    108–109
  enforcement of rules, 120–122
  exemptions, 106–109
  illegality, 106
  improving production or
    distribution of goods, 107
  inter–member trade, effect on,
    101–102
  minor agreements, 105–106
  predatory pricing, 116–117
  prevention of competition,
    102–104
  prohibition, 98–100
  restriction of competition,
    102–104
  severing illegal part of
    agreement, 108
  technical progress, promotion of,
    107
  within common market, 105
CONCENTRATIONS,
  abuse of dominant position,
    117–118

control under Regulation 4064/
  89, 118–120
CONFIDENTIALITY,
  access to measures adopted by
    Council, 20–21
CONTRIBUTORY NEGLIGENCE,
  damages, award of, 50
COUNCIL OF EUROPEAN UNION,
  adoption of measures, 17–19
  public access to measures
    adopted by, 20–21
COURT,
  mandatory references, 55–56
  reference under Article 177, 53
CULTURAL INTEGRATION,
  promotion of, 19–20
CURRENCY,
  export of, 74–75
CUSTOMERS,
  abuse of dominant position,
    115–116
CUSTOMS UNION,
  formation of, 59

DAMAGES,
  concurrent liability, 51
  contributory negligence, effect
    of, 50
  fundamental rights and general
    principles, protection of, 21
  loss of profits, for, 49
DECISIONS,
  direct effect of, 6–7
  jointly adopted by European
    Parliament and Council, 17
DEFENCE,
  enforcement proceedings, 31–32
  force majeure, 30–31
DIAMOND WORKERS' WELFARE SCHEME,
  funding, 59–60
DIRECT EFFECT,
  decisions, of, 6–7
  directives, of, 6–7
  horizontal, 7–8
  regulations, of, 6–7
  vertical, 7–8
DIRECTIVES,
  deadline for implementation,
    6–7
  direct effect of, 6–7

imprecisely worded, incorrect
implementation of, 13–14
jointly adopted by European
Parliament and Council, 17
non–implementation of, 11–12,
31–32
DISCRETIONARY REFERENCES,
court or tribunal, 53
mandatory references, 55–56
misuse of Article 177 procedure,
56–57
necessity, 53–54
tribunal, 53
validity, rulings on, 57–59
DOMESTIC PRODUCTS,
taxation of, 60–61

ECONOMIC ACTIVITY,
free movement of workers, 76
ECONOMIC AND MONETARY UNION
(EMU),
progress towards, 74–75
ECONOMIC ELEMENT,
freedom to provide services,
96–97
ECONOMIC POLICY,
legislative measure involving
choices of, 46–47
EDUCATION,
children of migrant workers,
84–85
discrimination in access to,
97–98
maintenance grant to cover,
83–84
qualifications, 92–93
EMPLOYMENT,
eligibility for, 80–81
equal pay. *See* EQUAL PAY
equality in, 81–82, 131–135
free movement of workers. *See*
WORKERS, FREE MOVEMENT OF
public service, in, 85–86
ENFORCEMENT OF E.C. LAW,
Article 169, actions under,
29–32
Article 170, actions between
Member States under, 32–33
Article 5, Member States'
obligations under, 28–29
competition rules, 120–122

expedited procedures, challenge
under Article 225 to use of, 34
illegal state aid, actions under
Article 93(2) on, 33–34
specific proceedings, 33–34
ENTRY,
workers, rights of, 79
ENVIRONMENT,
national strategies to protect,
64–65
EQUAL PAY,
direct discrimination, 126–127
equal work, for, 123, 129–130
indirect discrimination, 126–127
job classification scheme, 130–
131
occupational pensions, 125–128
part–time workers, 124–125
pay, meaning, 123–124
redundancy pay, 124–125,
128–129
work of equal value, 130–131
EQUAL TREATMENT,
employment, in, 81–82,
131–135
equal opportunities, 136–137
exceptions, 135–136
remedies, 135
social security, in, 131–132,
137–138
EQUALITY,
damages, claim for, 47
employment, in, 81–82,
131–135
equal pay. *See* EQUAL PAY
free movement of workers, 80
professional sporting activities,
regulation of, 81
recognition of principle of,
25–26
ESTABLISHMENT, RIGHT OF,
abolition of restrictions, 89–90
financial services, 91–92
qualifications, national
requirements on, 90–91
transitional period, 90
EUROPEAN ATOMIC ENERGY AUTHORITY
(EURATOM),
creation of, 1
EUROPEAN COAL AND STEEL
COMMUNITY (ECSC),
creation of, 1

EUROPEAN COMMUNITY (EC),
  breaches of law, state liability for, 12–13
  common market, establishment of, 3–4
  infringement of law, 14–15
  interim relief, granting of, 5–6
  legal order of, 1–15
  main institutions, 1
  new legal order, 3–15
  sovereign rights, permanent limitation of, 4–5
EUROPEAN CONVENTION ON HUMAN RIGHTS,
  general principles derive from, 21
EUROPEAN COURT OF JUSTICE (ECJ),
  action by European Parliament in, 16–17
  fundamental rights and general principles, protection of, 21–22
  misuse of Article 177 procedure, 56–57
  preliminary rulings under Article 177, 51–59
  prerogative of European Parliament, action to protect, 16
EUROPEAN ECONOMIC COMMUNITY (EEC),
  creation of, 1
EUROPEAN MONETARY UNION (EMU),
  opt out by U.K., 2
  provision for, 2
EUROPEAN PARLIAMENT,
  action in ECJ, 16–17
  failure to consult, 15–16
  prerogative, protection of, 16
EUROPEAN POLITICAL UNION (EPU),
  provision for, 2
EUROPEAN UNION (EU),
  legal order of, 1–15
  legal personality, 2
EXPEDITED PROCEDURES,
  challenge under Article 225 to use of, 34
EXPORTERS,
  monetary compensation amounts payable to, 47
EXPORTS,
  currency, of, 74–75

  derogations from Articles 30 to 34, 68–73
  health policy, risk relating to, 71
  humans, animals or plants, protection of, 70–71
  national treasures, protection of, 72
  public morality, restrictions on grounds of, 68–69
  public policy, restrictions on grounds of, 69
  restrictions on, 67–68

FAMILIES,
  free movement of workers and, 76–77
FAUTE DE PERSONNE,
  faute de service distinguished from, 45–46
FAUTE DE SERVICE,
  faute de personne distinguished from, 45–46
FINANCIAL SERVICES,
  right of establishment and provision of, 91–92
  single market in, 91
FISHING VESSELS,
  registration of, 90
FOODSTUFFS,
  permitted level of radioactive contamination in, 37–38
FORCE MAJEURE,
  Article 169, no defence to action under, 30–31
FREE MOVEMENT,
  capital, of, 73–75
  goods. *See* GOODS, FREE MOVEMENT OF
  workers. *See* WORKERS, FREE MOVEMENT OF
FUNDAMENTAL RIGHTS AND GENERAL PRINCIPLES,
  protection by ECJ, 21–22

GEOGRAPHICAL MARKET,
  identification of,113–114
GOODS, FREE MOVEMENT OF,
  Article 30, effect of, 61–67

charge disguised as tax or levy, 59–60

commercial property, protection of, 72–73

customs union, formation of, 59

derogations from Articles 30 to 34, 68–73

discriminatory taxation, 60–61

domestic products, taxation of, 60–61

environment, national strategies to protect, 64–65

exports, restrictions on, 67–68

health, risk to, 71

humans, animals or plants, protection of, 70–71

industrial property, protection of, 72–73

inter–member trade, measures not affecting, 66

measures having equivalent effect, 61–62

mutual recognition, principle of, 63–64

national products, promotion of, 62–63

national treasures, protection of, 72

public morality, restrictions on grounds of, 68–69

public policy, restrictions on grounds of, 69

public security, restrictions justified by, 69–70

quantitative restrictions, 61–68

Sunday trading, regulation of, 65

HEALTH. *See* PUBLIC HEALTH

HEARING,
right to, 26

HORIZONTAL DIRECT EFFECT,
creation of, 7–8

HUMANS,
protection of life and health of, 70–71

IMPORT LICENCES,
regulation of, 38–40

IMPORTS,

commercial property, protection of, 72–73

derogations from Articles 30 to 34, 68–73

hallmarking requirement, 66–67

health policy, risk relating to, 71

humans, animals or plants, protection of, 70–71

industrial property, protection of, 72–73

national products, promotion of, 62–63

national treasures, protection of, 72

public morality, restrictions on grounds of, 68–69

public policy, restrictions on grounds of, 69

INDIRECT EFFECT,
national law, interpretation of, 8–11

INDIVIDUAL,
Article 175, action for inactivity under, 42–43
compensation to, 46–47
effective judicial control, entitled to, 26–27
rule of law intended for protection of, 48–49

INDUSTRIAL PROPERTY,
imports or exports, restrictions on, 72–73

INDUSTRIAL SECRECY,
access to measures adopted by Council, 20–21

INSTITUTIONS,
Commission, 19–21
Council of European Union, 17–19
damages, 49–51
European Parliament, 15–17
liability of, 44–51
main, 1
non–contractual liability, 44–49

INTERGOVERNMENTAL CONFERENCE,
review of changes introduced by TEU, 2

INTERIM RELIEF,
application for, 32
granting of, 5–6
validity, rulings on, 57–59

INTERNAL MARKET,
   Council of European Union,
      measures adopted by, 18–19
INTERNATIONAL LAW,
   general principles derive from,
      21
INTERNATIONAL ORGANISATION,
   co–operation over problems
      relating to, 19–20

JOB CLASSIFICATION SCHEME,
   work of equal value,130–131
JUDICIAL CONTROL,
   effective, individual entitled to
      26–27
JUDICIAL PROCEEDINGS,
   Article 169, under, scope of,
      29–30
JUDICIAL REVIEW,
   Article 175, action for inactivity
      under 42–43
   Article 184, indirect challenge
      under, 43–44
   grounds for challenge, 41–42
   locus standi, 37–40
   non–reviewable acts, 36–37
   reviewable acts, 35–37

LEGAL CERTAINTY,
   damages, claim for, 47
   equality, 25–26
   legitimate expectations, 23–24
   non–retroactivity, 23
   proportionality, 24–25
LEGISLATION,
   liability for, Schoppenstedt
      formula, 46–47
LEGITIMATE EXPECTATIONS,
   challenge to EC legislation
      based on breach of, 23–24
   damages, claim for, 47
LIABILITY,
   concurrent, award of damages
      and, 50–51
   damages, for, 49–51
   E.C. institutions, of, 44–51
   legislation, for, 46–49
   non–contractual, 44–49
LOCAL AUTHORITY,

Sunday trading, regulation of,
   65
LOCUS STANDI,
   right to challenge, 37–38

MAASTRICHT TREATY,
   amendment of EEC Treaty, 1
   three–pillar structure created by,
      1–2
MAINTENANCE GRANT,
   education, 83–84
MATERNITY,
   women, protection of,133–134,
      136
MEDICAL SERVICES,
   freedom to receive, 96
MEMBER STATES,
   Article 170, actions under,
      32–33
   Article 5, obligations under,
      28–29
   breaches of EC law, liability for,
      12–13
   non–implementation of
      directive, 11–12, 31–32
   sovereign rights, permanent
      limitation of, 4–5
MERGERS,
   abuse of dominant position,
      117–118
MUTUAL RECOGNITION,
   principle of, 63–64

NATIONAL LAW,
   interpretation of, 8–11
NATIONAL PRODUCTS,
   promotion of, 62–63
NATIONAL TREASURES,
   exports or imports, restrictions
      on, 72
NATIONALITY,
   equality, recognition of principle
      of, 25–26
NECESSITY,
   preliminary ruling under Article
      177, 53–54
NEGLIGENCE,
   contributory, award of damages
      and, 50

NON-CONTRACTUAL LIABILITY,
   failure of administration, 45
   nature of, 44–45
   vicarious liability, 45–46
NON-PROFESSIONAL SERVICES,
   provision of, 95–96
NON-RETROACTIVITY,
   penal provisions, of, 23
NON-REVIEWABLE ACTS,
   examples, 36–37
NORTHERN IRELAND,
   effective judicial control,
      individual entitled to, 26–27

OCCUPATIONAL PENSION SCHEME,
   direct discrimination, 126–127
   equal rights to join, 127–128
   indirect discrimination, 126–127
   payments as pay, 125–126

PART-TIME WORKERS,
   redundancy pay, 124–125
   sick pay, entitlement to, 124
PAY,
   equal. *See* EQUAL PAY
   meaning, 123–124
PENAL PROVISIONS,
   non–retroactivity of, 23
PENSIONS. *See* OCCUPATIONAL PENSION
      SCHEME
PLANTS,
   protection of life and health of,
      70–71
PORNOGRAPHIC GOODS,
   quantitative restriction on
      import of, 61
PREGNANCY,
   women, protection of, 132–134,
      136
PRELIMINARY RULINGS,
   Article 177, under, 51–59
   discretionary references, 53–59
PRICING,
   predatory, 116–117
   unfair prices, 115–116
PRIVACY,
   access to measures adopted by
      Council, 20–21
PROCEDURAL RIGHTS,

effective judicial control, right
   to, 26–27
hearing, right to, 26
subsidiarity, 27–28
PRODUCT MARKET,
   identification of, 111–113
PROFESSIONAL QUALIFICATIONS. *See*
   QUALIFICATIONS
PROFESSIONAL RULES OF CONDUCT,
   residential requirements, effect
      of, 93
PROFITS,
   damages for loss of, 49
PROPORTIONALITY,
   damages, claim for, 47
   operation of, 24–25
PUBLIC BODY,
   enforcement of directive against,
      7–8
PUBLIC HEALTH,
   free movement of workers,
      restriction of, 86
   imports or exports, ban on, 71
PUBLIC INTEREST,
   access to measures adopted by
      Council, 20–21
PUBLIC MORALITY,
   imports or exports, restrictions
      on, 68–69
PUBLIC POLICY,
   concept of, 87
   free movement of workers,
      restriction of, 86–89
   imports or exports, restrictions
      on, 69
   misuse of Article 177 procedure,
      57
PUBLIC SECURITY,
   concept of, 87
   free movement of workers,
      restrictions on, 86–89
   imports or exports, restrictions
      on, 69–70
PUBLIC SERVICE,
   employment in, 85–86

QUALIFICATIONS,
   equivalence, 93–94
   harmonisation, 94
   national requirements on, 90–91

recognition, 93–94
services, provision of, 92–94

RADIOACTIVE CONTAMINATION,
foodstuffs, permitted level in, 37–38
REDUNDANCY PAY,
part–time workers, 124–125
pay, as, 128–129
REGULATIONS,
direct effect of, 6–7
indirect challenge under Article 184, 43–44
jointly adopted by E.P. and Council, 17
REMEDIES,
equal treatment principle, 135
REMUNERATION,
equal pay. *See* EQUAL PAY
services offered across national borders, 95–96
services provided for, 96–97
RESIDENCE,
separation of spouses, effect of, 78–79
services, provision of, 92–94
REVIEWABLE ACTS,
Article 173, action for annulment under, 35–37
examples, 36
RULE OF LAW,
individual, protection of, 48–49

SCHENGEN AGREEMENT,
incorporation in revised Treaty, 2
SCHOPPENSTEDT FORMULA,
liability for legislation, 46–49
SECONDARY LEGISLATION,
Article 5, Member States' obligations under, 28–29
SECURITY. *See* PUBLIC SECURITY
SERVICES,
cold calling, restriction on, 95–96
economic element, 96–97
educational, 97–98
financial, 91–92
freedom to receive, 96

medical, 96
non–professional, provision of, 95–96
qualifications, requirements relating to, 92–94
residential requirements, 92–94
tourists, 96
vocational training, 97–98
SEX,
equality, recognition of principle of, 25–26
SEX DISCRIMINATION,
employment, 132–135
SHOPS,
inter–member trade, selling arrangements not affecting, 66
sunday trading, regulation of, 65
SICK PAY,
part–time workers, 124
SINGLE EUROPEAN ACT (SEA),
amendment of EEC Treaty, 1
SOCIAL ADVANTAGE,
free movement of workers, 82–83
maintenance grant to cover education, 83–84
SOCIAL CHAPTER,
incorporation of, 2
opt out by U.K., 2
SOCIAL FIELD,
promotion of integration in, 19–20
SOCIAL SECURITY,
equal treatment, 131–132, 137–138
SOVEREIGN RIGHTS,
permanent limitation of, 4–5
SPORT,
professional activities, regulation of, 81
SPOUSES,
free movement of workers and, 77–79
residence rights, effect of separation on, 78–79
STATE AID,
illegal, action under Article 93(2) on, 33–34
STATE LIABILITY,
breach of EC law, for, 11–15
SUBSIDIARITY,

principle of, 27–28
SUNDAY TRADING,
　regulation of, 65

TAKEOVERS,
　abuse of dominant position,
　　117–118
TAXATION,
　charge disguised as tax or levy,
　　59–60
　discriminatory, 60–61
　domestic products, of, 60–61
　free movement of workers,
　　82–83
TORT,
　state liability for breach of E.C.
　　law, 15
TOURIST SERVICES,
　freedom to receive, 96
TRAINING. *See* VOCATIONAL TRAINING
TRANSPORT,
　failure to implement common
　　policy, 42–43
TREATY OF ROME,
　amendment of, 1
　creation of EEC, 1
TREATY ON EUROPEAN UNION. *See*
　　MAASTRICHT TREATY
TRIBUNAL,
　mandatory references, 55–56
　reference under Article 177, 53

UNFAIR PRICES,
　abuse of dominant position,
　　115–116

VALIDITY,
　rulings on, 57–59
VERTICAL DIRECT EFFECT,
　creation of, 7–8
VOCATIONAL TRAINING,
　children of migrant workers,
　　84–85
　discrimination in access to,
　　97–98
　equal treatment, 131–132
　meaning, 98
　qualifications, 92–93

WORKERS, FREE MOVEMENT OF,
　economic activity, 76
　education, 83–85
　eligibility for employment,
　　80–81
　entry, rights of, 79
　equality in employment, 81–82
　equality of treatment, 80
　family, 76–77
　maintenance grants and
　　education, 83–84
　public health, restriction on
　　grounds of, 86
　public policy, restriction on
　　grounds of, 86–89
　public security, restriction on
　　grounds of, 86–89
　public service, employment in,
　　85–86
　social advantages, 82–83
　spouses, 77–79
　tax advantages, 82–83
　worker, meaning, 75–76